GHOST
CATS *of*
THE
SOUTH

ALSO BY RANDY RUSSELL (WITH JANET BARNETT)

Ghost Dogs of the South

*The Granny Curse and Other Ghosts
and Legends from East Tennessee*

*Mountain Ghost Stories and
Curious Tales of Western North Carolina*

GHOST CATS *of* THE SOUTH

Randy Russell

JOHN F. BLAIR
PUBLISHER
Winston-Salem, North Carolina

JOHN F. BLAIR
PUBLISHER
1406 Plaza Drive
Winston-Salem, North Carolina 27103
www.blairpub.com

First John F. Blair Publisher hardcover edition October 2008

Manufactured in the United States of America

All photographs property of the author
Jacket and interior design by Debra Long Hampton

Library of Congress Cataloging-in-Publication Data

Russell, Randy.
    Ghost cats of the south / by Randy Russell.
        p.   cm.
    Companion to: Ghost dogs of the south.
    ISBN-13: 978-0-89587-360-6 (alk. paper)
    ISBN-10: 0-89587-360-5 (alk. paper)
 1. Animal ghosts. 2. Cats—Miscellanea. I. Title.
    BF1484.R868 2008
    398.20975'05—dc22   2008023025

Contents

Preface

~ ~ ~ ~

As a "ghostlorist" with three previously published titles in the field of Southern folklore, I am often asked whether or not I believe ghosts are real. Yes, I do. I have collected literally hundreds of first-person ghost experiences from across the South, encounters shared with me by the people who lived them. I have researched three hundred years of published folklore and have become familiar with the myths and legends of ghosts as well.

Sadly overlooked in published folklore are people's encounters with the ghosts of past family members of the four-legged variety. Conversely, visits from departed pets are easily the most common ghost experiences I hear when people share their real-life encounters with me. And cats refuse to be left out of most anything.

Cats are tied to place. No domestic animal is more territorial than the cat. When a cat moves in with a family, it likes to believe it has found a "forever home." *Forever* means just that to a cat.

Two rather famous cats vie for historical honors as the South's oldest example of a cat ghost.

The woodland beast that is half woman and half cat continues to be seen throughout the southern Appalachian Mountains. The fable of the Wampus Cat had its origin among the Cherokee of East Tennessee and western North Carolina at the time of the American Revolution.

A small cat is still seen today by visitors to an old Spanish fort in St. Augustine, Florida. The lithe animal was brought to America in the 1740s, according to legend. I am happy to share this well-established ghost cat in this collection.

In historical folklore, cats are often symbolic companions of witches. Cats see well at night. Witches want to. There are plenty of witches in the South, and I include in this collection more than one example of the continuing folk stories involving witches and their cats.

More important, perhaps, is the vast array of cat ghosts that populate our everyday lives. Many of the stories in this collection involve people just like us, and cats just like yours.

Ghosts hang around longer in the South than elsewhere. It's warmer here. The folklore is rich and fertile. All of the stories in this book are based on researched folklore of the South or were nurtured from the hundreds of ghost experiences shared with me by others when a comfortable corner, and a moment's confidentiality, could be found.

I would like to thank the North Carolina Center for the Advancement of Teaching in Cullowhee for regularly offering week-long seminars in folklore for the benefit of teachers across the state. I would also like to thank Cherokee artist and mask carver Davy Arch for his generosity in sharing the culture of his people and the stories told among his family and friends.

I thank the entire staff of John F. Blair, Publisher, in Winston-Salem. Blair published my first book, coauthored with my wife, Janet Barnett, in 1987. *Mountain Ghost Stories and Curious Tales of Western North Carolina* has remained in print since that time, due in no small part to the continuing enthusiasm of this important and historical publishing house for Southern folklore.

Finally, I would like to thank everyone who warmly and companionably provides a domestic cat with a forever home and a forever family. Cats are their own reward, of course. Just ask one.

I also need to offer a caveat to those who love cats no matter what they do. Ghost cats, like cats themselves, don't always behave the way we would want them to. In short, not all ghost cats are good ghosts. But all ghost cats have one thing in common. They exist.

GHOST
CATS *of*
THE
SOUTH

Chicken Soup Cat

"Oh, darn!" she said. "Arnie, we're out of gas again!"

The van heaved to a sputtering stop on a narrow Kentucky country road south of the interstate. It was a route Arnie had chosen on the spur of the moment to bypass traffic on the approach to Lexington. He and Pam were on their way to Florida and then back along the Gulf Coast to perform at the more crowded winter resorts. Arnie and Pam were street musicians, at least until they could get a song to take off on youtube.com and make money selling their CDs.

Arnie would get them there, to a place where they could perform one day as stage musicians to large, adoring crowds. Pam was sure of it. He was tall and handsome, with thick, curly hair. Arnie sang and played the sousaphone on the street.

Pam played accordion. He was thirty now. She was younger. They danced around and had fun with it.

They covered all the classic rock songs and could knock out a polka in a heartbeat. It was quite a show. People loved it. Arnie and Pam always made enough money to eat and pay their motel bill. Sometimes, they saved enough to rent a house in a tourist area and stay in one place for a while.

Arnie and Pam, trying to reach more people and see more places, had tried the Pacific Northwest for the summer. Pam was only a little pregnant when they left. Seattle was a bust, as was most of Oregon. The streets of the South were where a sousaphone-and-accordion band belonged. They had barely put back enough money for gas.

The couple had spent the trip thus far sleeping in the van at state parks along the way. And Pam found she needed more sleeping room. She'd never expected to be this big this soon. A sousaphone and an accordion take up a lot of space in a van. Not to mention Arnie, who slept sprawled out like a starfish.

And now this, out of gas on a twisting road somewhere on the short side of Lexington. They'd turned off Interstate 64 at a town called Jett and headed south on Highway 60, but it wasn't Highway 60 for long until it was something else. The nearest town now, according to the map, was Nonesuch. And the Kentucky River was just beyond. But neither Arnie nor Pam could tell exactly where they were by looking at the map. It wasn't like either one of them to pay attention to the odometer, for one thing. Or the fuel gauge.

Arnie threw up on the side of the road.

"Hey, I'm pregnant," Pam said. "I'm the one who's supposed to be doing that."

"Share and share alike," he said. "I think I have a fever. It hit me when I stood up from riding in the van. Might be this curvy road, though."

Pam laughed. "Nobody ever came straight home from anywhere on this road, that's a fact."

A man driving a pickup truck stopped. He had a can of gasoline in the bed of his truck. He told Arnie and Pam that the nearest town was Nonesuch and that they could find a gas station there. He asked where they were headed and where they were from.

"We're looking for a place to park for winter," Arnie said. "And a job, if you know of any."

Pam stared at him with her mouth open. *He must have a fever*, she thought. Sometimes, Arnie said things just to talk, but he never used the word *job* lightly. He'd be a father soon, and maybe that's what was messing him up.

The man told them he knew a place they could rent by the week, if they wanted.

"Better stay a night or two," the man said, "to see for sure." He winked at Pam.

They followed him along an old road to a little clapboard farmhouse. Then the man drove away, his arm out the window of his truck.

Pam turned the van in a circle in a front yard that was mostly weeds, then put it in reverse to back up to the porch. They heard a loud clunk, followed by two smaller clanks. The van wouldn't budge. The transmission had come apart, she guessed. Arnie wasn't good with cars, and neither was she.

The farmhouse was three rooms and a kitchen. Nothing much worked. The electricity was turned off. The propane tank was empty. But water flowed in the kitchen sink and the little bathroom. The living room had a fireplace, and Pam found a long stack of firewood along the south side of the house. Arnie moved the mattresses from the bedrooms and placed them side by side in front of the fireplace. Pam unzipped their sleeping bags and covered the mattresses.

Arnie was too sick in the morning to bring in firewood. They had some food in the van. Pam used a pan from the kitchen for coffee. She made bologna sandwiches. Four pieces of lunchmeat were left in the van. They had a jar of mustard. Arnie didn't want to eat. He seemed to have the flu. First chills, then fever, then chills again.

That night, Pam tried to make toast by putting the last slices of bread in a skillet and setting it in the fireplace. It worked. She placed the remaining two bologna slices in the skillet, too.

On her last trip for firewood, it was snowing, just enough to sprinkle her hair with tiny crystals. She didn't get the door quite closed. While she put their sandwiches together, a cat walked in. The room smelled like chicken soup.

"Hi, kitty," Pam said.

The cat meowed. It was a big, fat cat and didn't look hungry at all.

"I smell soup," Arnie said. He sat up on the mattress when the cat walked across him.

"So do I," Pam admitted. "I think it's the cat."

"Oh, the cat. I thought I was dreaming that."

The cat sat by Pam and watched the fire burn. She gave him a bit of fried bologna.

Pam played her accordion in her mind and sang out loud,

"My kitty has a first name, it's O-s-c-a-r."

She stroked the cat from his ears down his back. He was a big boy, about eighteen pounds, she guessed. His ears and head were scarred. A tough old guy.

"Oscar," she said, "you smell like chicken soup. How do you do that?"

He stroked his whiskers with his paw and didn't answer.

Arnie ate half his sandwich. The old tomcat rubbed against Pam's belly. He knew.

When she went to sleep, the cat was still there. When she woke up in the morning, he was gone.

"If I don't go get food, we're going to die."

"Soup," Arnie said. He was half asleep, still sick and weak. "Chicken soup."

"Yeah, you're going to die anyway," Pam teased. "And I'm naming the baby after the cat, not you."

"Soup," was all he said.

Pam got firewood first. The ground was blanketed in snow. Snow was in the trees. The world seemed silent in the snow. It seemed closer and smaller, as if the sky were on the ground and went only as high as the trees.

She cooked the last of the coffee. How could it be so cold so soon? *Kentucky may be in the South*, she thought, *but it isn't far enough south for me.*

Putting on all the clothes she could find, Pam discovered that her blue crocheted sweater reached only at the middle button now, between her breasts and belly. She was a different-sized person. She pulled on three pair of knee socks. The outer pair was red-and-white striped, the ones she wore for performing. If she froze to death in the woods, she would stick her feet in the air just before she died, so her body would be found sooner. She pulled her open sleeping bag off the mattress and wrapped it around her shoulders. It made a pretty good parka and kept her neck warm, too. It also fit easily around her stomach, and then some. Pam didn't need gloves, if she kept her hands rolled inside the edges of the sleeping bag.

If it's a boy, she thought, *I'm naming him Oscar. Middle name, Mayer.*

The cat was on the porch when she stepped outside in her winter-weather wardrobe. The daylight smelled like chicken soup. The outdoors looked pretty in snow. The big cat meowed and jumped off the porch in a trot.

Pam had no idea which way to go. She figured she would walk back to the main road and wait for a car to come by. Or perhaps she could figure out the way to Nonesuch. She didn't know.

The cat came back for her. He paced back and forth in front of the porch. Pam smelled chicken soup again. And just like that, the cat was off again.

"Okay," she said, "let's go."

She followed the cat. And the smell of chicken soup. Hot soup. It was just the thing for snow.

By the time they reached a road, Pam's shoes were soaked and her feet were cold. Her socks were wet almost to her knees from walking in snow. At least it had stopped snowing and there was little or no wind. The exercise kept her warm. She had to hurry to keep up with the cat. If they weren't going to town, they were going somewhere, she supposed. That old cat had to live somewhere. It had a collar, after all.

Pam watched the ground, following the cat tracks. Every

time she stopped and looked up to see where they were going, the big tomcat stopped, but only for a moment, to make sure she was there. Then he took off. Eventually, she looked up and couldn't see him anymore. But the tracks were there. And the smell of chicken soup.

She heard the sound of a door closing.

There it was. A roadside café. It had a row of windows in front and lights on inside. The windows looked steamy. Smoke rose from the vent on the roof. One car was in the parking lot. The sign over the front door said the café was the Yellow Cat Diner. Cat tracks led to the front door. The whole place smelled like chicken soup.

The man inside wore a white T-shirt and an apron and had a faded tattoo of an anchor on his forearm. He wore a paper hat on his head. The tomcat sat on the counter. A pie was inside a small display case. Bacon sizzled on the grill. A jukebox sat just inside the door.

"Morning, miss," he said. "Take off your shoes and sit in that last booth by the gas heater. You can prop your feet up there. Did you follow the cat here?"

"Yes." Pam smiled, letting the sleeping bag slip from her shoulders.

"Two eggs or three?" the man asked. "Do you like them with the yolks runny?"

Later, they rode in his car out to the little dilapidated farmhouse and brought Arnie back to the café. The place was empty when they left, except for the cat.

"We have to hurry directly back," the man told them. "The customers will be coming in soon. I have some things there for the flu. You can go to town later. Hope you don't mind."

Pam and Arnie didn't mind at all. Anyplace warm would do. Anyplace with food.

"Soup?" Arnie asked.

"Yeah, we got soup. Hamburgers and chili, too. We'll get awful busy here shortly. Got breaded tenderloins in the freezer, you want something fancy. And I know somebody who'll come out and look at your van. See what it needs and all."

It was busy, all right. Workmen came into the café in a steady march. They came in staggered shifts from a road-building crew. The man behind the counter couldn't keep up. Arnie curled up in the last booth, his feet stuck out in front of the gas heater. The cat sat on the Formica tabletop and watched the crowd.

Pam carried plates and bowls of food from the kitchen to the counter and out to the booths. Customers ordered by saying out loud what they wanted, then found a seat. Somehow, the man in the paper hat and stained apron got all the orders right. The café was packed. Pam carried empty dishes back to the kitchen. The men left change for her on the tables and the counter.

"Never seen a pregnant waitress in socks before and no shoes," one of them said.

"Never seen a man eat horse-meat chili before and like it," Pam said back to him. "You going to want hay after you finish that?"

The whole place laughed. Someone started the jukebox. Pam sang along as she worked.

The jukebox played old songs, ones you heard a hundred times growing up as a kid. The records hadn't been changed in years.

Arnie felt better, listening to the old songs. And he felt much better than that after two bowls of chicken soup. He got up eventually and wandered into the kitchen and started doing dishes.

He and Pam stayed through Christmas. The man who lent them the gasoline and let them stay in the little farmhouse was a regular customer. They settled up the rent at the end of the week, and every week thereafter. Friday and Saturday nights, Pam and Arnie played live music. Soon, the Yellow Cat Diner was as busy at suppertime as it was at lunch.

Each night when the café closed, Arnie played taps on the sousaphone, then did the pots and pans. Once they were cleaned, he used them to play the drums. He set a pot upside down on the floor and banged it with his foot and mimicked playing the sousaphone with his hands. *Just might work*, he thought.

Arnie and Pam got to know everyone who came in. There was the shade-tree mechanic who ordered the used parts for Arnie's van, and the two local boys who helped him get the gears in place. And the nurse from the county hospital who assisted Pam with prenatal care and carefully monitored her pregnancy. Pam delivered food to the tables three times a day with a thermometer in her mouth. Her tips were always larger then.

There were the father and son who brought more firewood out to the farmhouse and loaned Pam and Arnie coal-oil lamps so they had lights at night. They lived on a farm that touched the river, they said.

And there was the high-school girl who sewed clothes and cut Arnie's hair. She had red-apple cheeks and curly blond hair.

She adjusted Pam's skirt waists. She created pleats in Pam's tops by stitching in extra pieces of cloth and knotting a sewn thread at the top of each fold.

By January, Pam was too big to play the accordion. Her feet were tired. She and Arnie talked it over. It was time to go. When a break in the winter weather came, they loaded their things in the van for one last day at the café.

Arnie talked to the owner of the café before they left.

"She wants to have the baby on down south," he said. "It's warmer down there, you understand? And we'll be closer to kin."

"You have enough money to find a place?"

"Yes, sir, thanks to you."

"No, don't be saying that. You two made me more money by working here than you made for yourself. I have a little cash bonus for you. I've been saving up. For the baby, you see?"

The cook took off his paper hat to say goodbye to Pam. He handed her an envelope. Pam put it in her purse.

"Thank you," she said.

She hugged the cat goodbye and sang it the Oscar Mayer song. He seemed to like it. One ear twitched the whole time.

They drove away to buy a full tank of gas for the road.

"Arnie," she said from the passenger seat, "you smell like chicken soup."

They stopped for gas in Nonesuch. Inside the filling station, Pam stocked up on a few things for the trip. She bought four bags of corn chips, six Hostess Sno Ball cupcakes, and a jar of pickles.

"Are you the couple been staying at the old farmhouse up the hill?" the clerk asked.

"Yes, we are," Pam said. "It will be empty now, if you know anyone who needs a place to rent."

"Oh, it's never empty long," the clerk told her. "Don't know why, but someone's always living in that house. Not locals much, though. Just folks the cat dragged in."

"The tomcat that smells like chicken soup?"

The clerk stared at her a moment.

"No, ma'am," he said. "It's just an expression. You know, what the cat dragged in?"

Pam nodded. She reached into her purse to get money and pulled out the envelope from the café.

Arnie came over from the men's room to help her carry their purchases.

"Have you ever eaten at the Yellow Cat Diner?" he asked the clerk. "You know, if it wasn't for that diner, we wouldn't have lived through December. My wife and I both worked there."

The clerk cocked his head.

"The food is the best there is," Arnie added. "You should tell people to go there."

Pam pulled another envelope from her purse. And then another one.

"Did you say the Yellow Cat Diner?" the clerk asked. "You worked there *this* winter?"

"That would be the one and only," Arnie said cheerfully. "It's right up the road a ways. Tell people to go there, now. It's real home cooking and all. Ask for the chicken soup. You'll like it a lot, I promise you."

Still more envelopes were in her purse. Pam eventually found her own money. She got it out and crammed all the envelopes back in. There must have been one for every week they'd worked at the café.

"Oh, I'd tell people about it, if it was still there," the clerk said. "The Yellow Cat Diner burned down when I was a little boy. Nothing is there now. Nothing has been there since the fire."

"Naw," Arnie said. "We were there just a bit ago. The place is hopping."

"Not the Yellow Cat Diner. You've been somewhere else."

Once their purchases were in the van, Arnie ran back to the store. He stepped inside and stood with his hand on the door.

"I'm going to draw you a map," he said. He pointed at the clerk and smiled. "I'm going to draw you a map and bring it right back."

The clerk laughed. "Why don't you take one of these disposable cameras and get me a picture while you're at it?"

"Okay. How much are they?"

"On the house," the clerk said.

He tossed one to Arnie from the counter display. Arnie caught it in one hand and was out the door.

Riding back to the farmhouse road, Pam counted the envelopes and then took the money out of each one.

"Arnie?"

"Save me that envelope, darling," he said. "I think there's a pen in the glove box."

"*Arnie!*"

"Yes, dear?"

"I've got more than six thousand dollars here. My purse was full of those envelopes, and I swear he gave me only one."

The cat walked the counter at the Yellow Cat Diner. A large pot of chicken soup bubbled on the stove. Sliced carrots rose to the surface, then dove back in. The broth thickened.

The cook came around to the counter with a ladle in his hand. The same pieces of pie were inside the display as had been there the day Pam walked in wearing a sleeping bag over her blue crocheted sweater, her red-and-white-striped socks soaked with the first snow of the season. He leaned his elbows on the counter, his face next to the cat. They both looked out the window as the van drove slowly past. They could see Pam in the passenger seat. But she couldn't see them. She couldn't see anything there at all.

The big tomcat flipped his tail each time the van went by.

"Well, I need another waitress now," the man in the paper hat said to the cat. "Go see what you can do."

Slivers of Bone

≈ ≈ ≈ ≈ ≈ ≈ ≈ ≈ ≈ ≈ ≈ ≈ ≈ ≈ ≈

Wampus Cat lives wild in the Southern woods yet today. She is not a house cat.

Wampus Cat is a bad cat. The size and weight of a full-bodied woman, she walks upright on cat feet. She rambles through the rhododendron hells of darkened mountain coves, paces silently under the canopy of tall pines and hardwoods.

Her scream, like that of a mountain panther, is heard from time to time echoing eerily in the middle of the night along the spine of the southern Appalachian Mountains. Residents of mountainous Georgia, North Carolina, and Tennessee will tell you Wampus Cat originated among the eighteenth-century Cherokee.

Half beast, half woman, she is old and she is young. She

has human eyes and a human brain, with the feral heart and the appetite of a wild cat. Wampus Cat adapts. She forever changes and is forever hungry. She eats men.

She wears a tail. Where Wampus Cat hunts in the mountainous woods, she leaves behind only a scattering of white slivers of bone on the forest floor. Sometimes, the bones are those of a human. She carries with her the lingering scent of sudden death.

Wampus Cat rapidly devours all she catches, hair, skin, and flesh. She consumes eyes, nose, and ears. She feeds on organs and fingertips. She gobbles feet, ankles, shins. She gulps down hands, wrists, elbows. She sucks in the skin, the meat, the tendons, the bones. Wampus Cat snaps ribs in two in her teeth and swallows both ends. In eating her stunned catch, Wampus Cat coats her own face, her chest, her fists of claw and fur with blood. Little pieces of bone fall from her carnivorous mouth as she feeds.

Along the Blue Ridge Mountains, in the Great Smoky Mountains National Park, in the Joyce Kilmer Memorial Forest and the Nantahala National Forest, she eats quickly and slips back into the shadows of rocks and tall trees. She moves to a mountain stream and washes the blood from her fur, her claws, her breasts.

Cherokee lore tells of two animals known as Long Tail. One is the possum. The other is the half-woman, half-cat mountain creature known today as Wampus Cat. The Cherokee expression for Wampus Cat may be spoken only by witches, and it will not be repeated here. The phrase is too dangerous to say out loud by those untrained in the furthermost reaches of native spiritual medicine.

Modern Cherokee people rarely admit to having witches in their culture, and certainly not in their own communities. Cherokee witches are men. They have existed since the beginning, skilled in a magic so dark that it is forbidden among Cherokee to ever say that anyone is a witch. A curse will fall on the person who says it. The Cherokee do not like to believe they have ever met or been in the company of such a man.

The Cherokee witch will never tell another person that he is one. Were he discovered, he would be put to death. He wears no outward sign of his secret familiarity with the darkest of conjuring arts, arts that can transform man into beast and beast into man. A Cherokee witch will never tell on himself, even to his own family. Most Cherokee today do not admit that they have even heard of the existence of a witch among them. But they know better.

In the 1700s, the Cherokee more openly tolerated the practice of dark arts by a few elders of the council governments. Conjures, especially war rituals, were never revealed to women. To do so would weaken the strength of Cherokee magic. Such magic was crucial in times of war. English soldiers burned Cherokee towns to the ground in the 1700s. It was the failure of the sacred magic that allowed this to happen.

When the forced colonization of the Southern territories reached into the mountains, it was a crisis for all Native Americans living there. To keep the Cherokee from joining the colonists in the Revolutionary War, the British destroyed their towns at will. Despite agreements to stay out of the conflict, the Cherokee Nation came under relentless and unprovoked attacks by soldiers of the English crown.

This was a period when the sacred rituals had to be

protected at all costs. It was a very risky time for a Cherokee woman to wonder about conjuring.

One young Cherokee bride, however, was overly curious about all things concerning her new husband. In her case, curiosity didn't kill the cat, although she may have wished it had.

British soldiers, cutting wide swaths of destruction and subjugation among the Native Americans, were making their way through the fertile mountain valleys along the Tuckasegee River in the Cherokee Nation. They burned towns and crops well into what is now mountainous Jackson County, North Carolina, approaching the future location of the town of Cherokee itself.

Important councils were held in secret among the men of all Cherokee communities. Emissaries traveled from council to council with the most recent reports of destruction, sparing no detail in telling of the relentless atrocities suffered at the hands of English soldiers. American history contains few accounts of the ruin wreaked upon the Cherokee Nation by the British. But the stories live on among the Cherokee. Town sites that were burned, some repeatedly, by the British are well known to Cherokee cultural keepers such as Davy Arch.

Davy Arch tells his native stories and presents lectures on Cherokee history and culture on a regular basis for the North Carolina Center for the Advancement of Teaching in Cullowhee. Skilled in stone carving, basket making, flint knapping, and Cherokee traditional cooking, Davy is best known as a master mask carver.

Early in life, Davy Arch and his family lived with his grandfather, who taught the young boy the Cherokee stories, the practice of herbal medicine, and the harvesting of wild plants for food. They lived on Stilwell Branch in the Painttown community on the Qualla Boundary. His education in Cherokee culture continued after graduation from high school in 1975, when he went to work at the Oconaluftee Indian Village and Living History Museum. There, Davy learned his true calling and was taught by elder Sim Jessan how to carve masks of native wood. From other elders, he learned the meaning of a variety of masks. Davy continues to study older masks tied to stories almost entirely forgotten by the generations.

Besides the traditional masks used in Cherokee dance for centuries, Davy carves story masks entirely of his own pattern. These original works of art, designed to hold a particular Cherokee story or myth, are elegant and alluring aids in his retelling of the Cherokee stories. A mask carved by Davy Arch holds magic. So do the original masks of the Cherokee.

Davy carves masks of buckeye wood, cherry, pine, and walnut. His masks have been displayed at the Kennedy Center in Washington, D.C. His stories have been published in the award-winning book *Living Stories of the Cherokee*. As a participant for six years in the North Carolina Arts Council's Visiting Artist Program, he has presented programs on Cherokee culture in schools throughout North Carolina. Additionally, he has presented at the North Carolina Museum of History, at the North Carolina Museum of Art, at the annual Symposium on the American Indian in Tahlequah, Oklahoma, and on National Public Radio. A member of the board of directors of the Qualla Arts and Crafts Mutual, he has also demonstrated his craft at numerous arts festivals, including the

1982 World's Fair in Knoxville. His earliest recognition was a Grand Prize for carving at the Cherokee Indian Fair in 1979, four years after graduating high school.

On a walk in the area of Judaculla Rock, deep in a green cove along a creek feeding the Tuckasegee River, just beyond a turnoff of rural Caney Fork Road, Davy Arch points out features of the Cherokee town that once occupied the area and was burned at least twice by the British in the 1700s. The town site is a few miles from East Laport, North Carolina.

It was here Wampus Cat was born.

On a chilly October day, Davy uses his pocketknife to split river cane growing along the water's edge to demonstrate how Cherokee baskets begin. He speaks of the season as a time of harvesting chestnuts, an important food source. The American chestnut is now entirely gone. Davy Arch is accustomed to seeing things that aren't there any longer.

He finds an outcropping of soapstone and runs his hands over a curved indentation where a piece was two centuries before hewn away. Davy describes the size and shape of the soapstone bowl that isn't there, carefully surveying the age-old tool marks where the bowl was first cut into shape and then removed whole. And then he sees where another was cut away.

"This area of soapstone," he says, looking up a rising ridge of outcroppings above the creek, "is one of the best I have seen for a Cherokee town. A soapstone bowl large enough to hold a man was found turned upside down in the rocks of the creek not so long ago."

The huge bowl had been moved by flood, and the priceless native artifact hid from discovery in plain view for decade after decade by being upside down among other sizable stones in the bed of a rapidly flowing mountain creek. Davy notes that the size of the bowl is clear evidence of communal food preparation in Cherokee towns.

Judaculla Rock is a state historical site. Every year, hundreds of people visit the large rock carved with ancient native shapes and figures. The original meaning of the carvings in the rock has been lost to time. Some believe they are a map of a road through ancient tribal lands. Some believe the deeply incised figures represent the hunt, important battles, daily Native American life. Others believe Judaculla Rock is where the spirit of the hunt returned to physical form as a slant-eyed giant and left carved instructions for entry into the Cherokee spirit world.

Few visitors to Judaculla Rock ever see the town that isn't there, unless someone like Davy Arch is along to point it out to them. Perhaps overgrown with trees or river cane, perhaps at the edge of the valley pasture along the road to Judaculla Rock, the burned foundation of a Cherokee house from the 1700s rests undiscovered, hidden by soil and time. It is the house where a bride lived with her hunter husband before the town was burned to the ground by the British and the people fled.

"I must know," she told her husband. "I must know what you do and say when the women aren't allowed."

Her husband wouldn't tell her. This made her jealous. A husband should tell his wife everything.

"I must know!" she said. "It isn't fair!"

He left for the secret council held that night at a campfire somewhere in the woodland above the town. The autumnal council was a serious one. The location was near a sacred tree. The men would discuss the possibility of relocating the people from the town as the British soldiers advanced. The elders would ask the spirit world to come close within the circle of their earth world. It was a solemn time, and helpers in the Cherokee spirit world were needed for guidance. The men would dance to bring the spirit world closer. They would sing the sacred songs.

"I must know," she said. "And I will."

She had already made her plans. At dusk, she retrieved the panther skin from where she had hidden it and followed her husband. The panther hide was her father's. The bride had borrowed it from his house earlier in the day, when no one was there. She would wear it once she entered the dark woods. If any man attending the council caught a glimpse of her, he would think he saw an animal in the darkness, and the council would continue.

The Cherokee woman would keep her distance, coming just close enough to hear what was said when the men gathered. They gossiped about the women, she guessed. They said horrible things about the women and shared secrets among themselves that only a husband should be allowed to know. They laughed at the women. Why else would no women be allowed at councils?

If her husband spoke of her to the other men, she would kick him out of her house. If he dared say to others that he was not happy with her for any reason, their marriage would be over. She would see to it. But for now, she simply had to know.

What if her husband said another woman was prettier?

"I must know," she said softly as she walked.

In the darkened woods, she pulled the panther skin over her shoulders and purposely lagged far behind. She heard the drums. The council fire would be easy to find. She heard voices ahead of her greeting each other, as the path turned one way and then the next to avoid rocks and trees. The bride caught her toe on a root and turned off the path to wait in the darkness, the fire just ahead.

She waited until the drumming and the dances were through, until the chants rose to summon the spirits for protection. Then came silence, and the men began to speak. Creeping closer, she heard an elder's voice, then others speaking in turn. The men spoke urgently but in low voices. The words were hard to make out. She had to know what they were saying and so moved closer. Twigs snapped under her feet.

"Aey-aey wah!"

There was a sudden cry at her side. A sentinel rushed her and was upon her, pushing her powerfully forward. She was propelled against her will, pushed along too quickly to react. She lurched forward, stumbled, got up, and was pushed again. And again.

The sacred tree rose behind her at the forest edge. She fell on all fours within the circle of men, bruising her hands and knees. Gasping, the bride clung to the panther skin that covered her, the tail falling between her legs. The men quickly stood, staring at the sudden and curious interruption of their council work. Only the elders stayed seated.

Her face illuminated in the firelight, the bride was recognized in a moment. She was equally recognized as a woman who had broken her cultural duty and who spied upon her own people. The woman had transgressed the honor of every man in the council, of every man in the town, of every man in the Cherokee Nation. She had trespassed on the path occupied by spirits.

She stood, still clutching the panther skin. She grabbed breaths as quickly as she could, her heart pounding like that of a captured animal. No one moved to help her. She stood alone within the circle of men.

Her husband stared at her in awestruck fear. He was in love with all his heart, but this act was dire. It could not go unpunished. As her pleading eyes found him, he turned away. His bride would be ostracized. He was certain of it. The question he now considered was whether or not he would leave with her, whether or not he would keep with his wife and leave his family behind, his people.

She looked for her father. She could not find him. He had turned his back in horror and shame, having recognizing his daughter before most of the others did.

A voice rose in sudden anger and cursed the bride. It was one of the elders. The elder was a witch, but this was unknown to the others. It was unknown to his family. To be a witch among the Cherokee was to hold a secret known only to one.

The spirit world was close that night. The witch cursed the woman in a manner he probably shouldn't have. His angry prayer turned the woman into what she wore. The panther skin became her skin at the moment he spoke. The panther tail became her tail. The panther paws became her paws.

A prayer drum began to sound, and another in unison. A second elder, one who recognized black magic when he saw it, called out for the woman panther to leave. She must leave at once. As the bride became as much cat as woman, she grew into a violent threat to men.

"Leave us! Leave forever and live at night!"

The bride didn't know it yet, but she possessed the power to kill and consume men.

"Leave us!" another of the elders cried. "Leave us forever." He called the panther woman Long Tail instead of using her name. It was the bride's father.

"Leave us," the young husband said. "Leave us forever."

Wampus Cat walked away from the burning fire and sounding drums, walked away into the night woods, walked away from her people, walked away from the men. Throughout the night, a panther scream was heard from the steep hills rising above the river cane, above the rushing mountain water in the rocky stream. An Appalachian panther scream, it is said, sounds like the scream of a woman. This one did.

Wampus Cat wandered in a daze, coming to terms with her two selves, with woman and cat, one as feral as the other. She had been reborn into something wild.

Bewitched by a magic she didn't comprehend, Wampus Cat learned the life of a carnivore in the woods. She could not eat chestnuts. She could not eat blueberries. She killed small woodland creatures and devoured them. One morning before sunrise, she found a sleeping deer. She leapt upon it and subdued it quickly, drawing blood with her panther claws, inflicting fatal injury with her teeth and jaws on the animal's writhing neck.

Her town moved during the next few weeks, leaving behind Judaculla Rock, the fertile valley, the river cane, the soapstone cliff ledges, and the rushing mountain stream. The people carried food and belongings, seeking refuge from the coming British troops. The town stood empty the day it was burned.

Attracted by the only society she knew, Wampus Cat followed the Cherokee. She stayed nearby. She saw hunters in the woods from time to time and followed them.

One day, she allowed a youthful hunter to come too close. When he saw her panther skin moving through the woods, she became his prey. She rushed away, but he followed her.

Confounded by loneliness, by her misfortune to be shunned and unloved, Wampus Cat let him come near. She stood on two legs and watched his approach. The hunter was confused. He was yet a boy of only fourteen and not a member of the council of men. He drew his arrow and stared to where it would in an instant fly. He raised his aim to the animal's chest and saw the bride's twin woman's breasts. And then he saw her face.

Wampus Cat stood still and waited. Her belly moved with her breathing. Her tail twitched.

The youth was horrified. He dropped his bow and his arrows and ran away.

She wept.

Then she screamed.

Word spread quickly of the young hunter's experience. He could say little about what he had seen, but the effect was obvious to everyone. He could not sleep. The fourteen-year-old wandered among the people during the day, eating from meals that were prepared for others. He refused to keep himself washed. Seeing a creature half woman and half cat had damaged his spirit. The young man could not bring himself to hunt again. He would no longer go into the woods alone.

"She will not stay away from us," an elder said.

"She will steal the children next," said another. "A married woman without children will long for them."

"She will not leave us."

"We could kill her," a third joined in.

"She can be killed only by halves. One half keeps the other half alive. The cat survives the woman and brings the woman back to life. The woman survives the cat and brings the panther back to life. You cannot kill an animal that is two separate things."

"Then we must make her leave."

The husband was chosen. He would go into the woods and call her name and frighten her away. The husband was instructed to fast in preparation.

"I will go insane," he told the elders. "I will let my people down. If I see her, I will go insane."

"We will protect you. We have found a way. She is in love with you, and that is the strongest power over her that we possess. It is the power of the spirit and of the earth both. Love is made of sky and of mud."

The husband nodded. The elders knew best. He would not argue. "How will you protect me?"

"A mask is being made. It is carved of two woods and joined. One half is cat, and one half is devil. The mask will protect you, and it will also frighten her away. She will not see you through the mask. She will see herself instead. She will see how hideous she has become, and she will never desire to be seen by her people again."

Panther screams were heard every night until the mask

was finished. One half was maple, with human eyes. It was interlocked with carved dovetails into the bottom half of walnut. The bottom half had an animal nose and a crooked, open mouth full of sharp teeth and tongue. The mouth was dyed the color of blood. Whiskers were carved from the center outward and dyed black. The center of the mouth just above the tongue was open. Wearing the mask, the husband could call out to his bride.

The husband walked the hills in darkness without a weapon. The mask would protect him from all things wild. It was a powerful magic, the most powerful yet created by his people.

Soon, he heard the scream, and he followed the horrifying echo on narrow paths into the night woods. Wearing the mask, he seemed to see clearly at night. He found his way easily, quietly, until he was near enough. The husband called out his bride's name. His voice sounded like a screeching owl, or worse. It was not a human sound when he spoke through the mask. The magic was strong.

Wampus Cat came to him. She circled at a distance, moving from tree to tree until she was behind him. Mountain panthers hunt from behind.

He called her name again. It was the scream of an animal.

She answered him. She called softly, trying to speak.

He turned slowly around, fearful of the half-beast that was now directly behind him. She expected to see the beloved face of her husband and saw the hideous mask instead. In the winter moonlight, through leafless trees to one side of a tall stand of pines, she saw herself instead of his face. Her tail lifted. The muscles in her legs tightened, ready to spring.

This time when he spoke, he spoke in words.

"This is you," he said. "Look at my face. This is you."

Wampus Cat stared. She waited. Blood rushed to her head, to her heart, and back again.

"You are hideous," he told her. "Look at my face. You are hideous and must leave my people be. You are not one of us. You must leave all Cherokee. This mask is you. This is what we see when we see you. Go! You shall never want us to see you again. You are hideous."

Wampus Cat rushed away into the night. She learned the look of the mask, which was now her own appearance. She lived in the woods alone. She moved away from the Cherokee, from all Cherokee, higher into the mountains, where fewer people lived.

Over the years, she was drawn to farms and homes of settlers. They were not Cherokee. Occasionally, one of them came upon her in the woods. She let them when they did, when their paths crossed. One man with a gun saw her in a tree. He was with a hound. When the man looked up at Wampus Cat, he saw her face. It was hideous. He was frozen to that spot upon seeing her. He could not shoot. He could not flee.

She hissed at the dog. It tucked tail and ran away.

Fur flying through air, from lofty perch to forest floor, Wampus Cat was on the man in seconds. She pinned him on his back to the ground. He wanted to scream, urgent to push back up at her, to get her off somehow. It was useless. He was done before he could begin. She covered him and writhed, her claws opening his chest. Her hind legs held him flush against the involuntary thrusts of his hips and legs. Long white panther teeth sliced into his neck and found a warm bath of spurting blood. Wampus Cat devoured him. He was not Cherokee.

She ate the soft parts first, the organs and appendages. She ate his face. She separated his arms and legs with tooth and razor claw. Wampus Cat ate all of him, leaving behind a small scattering of white slivers of human bone.

As far as anyone at home knew, the man had walked into the woods one day and never returned.

Over the decades, Wampus Cat has been seen as far south as the Georgia mountains, as far north as the wooded hills in West Virginia. She has been seen by hikers on the Appalachian Trail, always in the mountains along either side of the rugged border between North Carolina and Tennessee. According to all reports, she is seen from a distance, a walking panther in the mountain woods, a flash of disappearing fur among the trees. When Wampus Cat is seen up close, no one is left alive to report the occurrence.

In recent years, sightings of Wampus Cat have been reported by the influx of tourists and campers visiting the Smoky Mountains by way of Gatlinburg, Tennessee. Others have reported seeing Wampus Cat close to centers of population. She has even been reported, on rare occasions, haunting the underground tunnels at the University of Tennessee in Knoxville.

The college accounts are likely urban myth. The lithe Wampus Cat avoids people, especially in groups. When paths cross in the upland woods, among the mists that rise where streams change into waterfalls, she can't help herself. It is her nature to eat, just as it is her nature to never die. The woman walks the woods; but when it comes to food, the panther decides.

Campers, day bikers, and long-distance hikers in the remote reaches of the southern Appalachian Mountains should know that whenever a small scattering of bone is found on the forest floor, it is best not to linger. It is best to keep moving and to keep your head down. Wampus Cat will let you move on as long as you don't see her face. It is hideous. And it is magic. It will freeze you where you stand.

A temporary haunt of Wampus Cat is easily identified. The tourist brochures and hiking guides do not warn of this singular hazard. If you plan on camping in the Smoky Mountains overnight, it is best to stay away from any found, or yet unfound, scattering of bone. The next little pile of skeletal remains among the hemlocks in the mountain forest may be your own.

Garden Cat

~~~~~~~~~~~~~~~~~

When Dr. Hooper Lear met his yellow cat, Cleo, he met a friend for life. And beyond.

An avid gardener since his retirement from dentistry, Hooper devoted much of his free time to his large front and back gardens in his suburban Williamsburg home. In a few years, his gardens were the pride of the neighborhood. Small weddings from the local Episcopal church were occasionally held in his backyard. The garden arch was covered with fragrant climbing roses throughout the late spring and summer, perpetual bloomers carefully selected and perfectly groomed by Hooper himself.

Hooper's back garden was almost an entire acre, with two in-ground water treatments, including a favored koi pond, and winding paths through a wide variety of decorative and blooming plants and shrubs. He was drawn to the koi pond, where he often plotted his day of a morning. The sound of the circulating water from two strategically placed pumps was soothing and tranquil, as was the constantly changing surface of watercress. The colorful koi, spotted black and red and orange and white, balanced like birds in nearly motionless flight within the current.

Because Hooper had come to gardening late in life, he laid out the design beforehand, careful to leave strolling areas and open spaces large enough for casual use. His wide stone path to the large rose arch provided perfect protection from soil and grass for the swishing hems of bridal gowns. A few of the fuller wedding gowns seemed not to move at all as the brides walked down the aisle, reminding Hooper of the seemingly motionless koi swimming in place against the current of the circulating water.

Although he hadn't designed the garden for weddings in particular, Hooper was always delighted when ceremonies were held there. He began to experiment with different bulb plants to provide more dramatic and lasting color throughout the summer. Nearsighted since childhood, the retired dentist always wore glasses. He needed a magnifying glass in addition when studying the catalogs of bulb plants.

He sat on the stone bench by the koi pond among the irises and laid out his garden in his head. Hooper wanted all the paths lined with bulbs. But his first few plantings were dismal failures. He learned quickly that bulbs, tulip bulbs in particular, had a natural enemy in Williamsburg. Squirrels dug them up when he wasn't looking, carried them off, and replanted them, burying them as food to be retrieved in winter.

The replanting was as annoying as the outright theft. Hyacinths and daffodils popped up in spring everywhere but where Hooper had planted them. He learned that squirrels also cut blooming tulips and carried off the flowers. He had no idea why. They didn't seem to eat them. They just liked taking them, was all.

He decided on screen. He planted his first several bulbs and laid down heavy screen on the soil to keep the squirrels from digging. Of course, the screen would need to be lifted in spring, and it looked pretty awful there on top of the soil in winter. It also had to be cut around the perennials, then held in place with stones. It was ugly, but nothing else seemed to work. He'd tried a squirrel feeder or two. Supposedly, feeding the squirrels would distract them from stealing garden plantings. Nope. He just had more squirrels showing up.

Somehow, when no one was watching, the squirrels got under the screen and dug up his plantings. Sometimes, the bulbs were left strewn about. Perhaps the squirrels just wanted to make sure he wasn't planting something they actually wanted. He planted the bulbs again, and the squirrels dug them up again.

Still, Hooper was intent on a major planting of bulbs that autumn. Lilies and daffodils, narcissi and tulips. Especially blue scilla, and the dramatic fritillaria varieties from Turkey. How could he grow a proper garden without fritillaria bells? A garden needed its surprises or it wasn't really a garden to begin with. He added two allium sparkler varieties to his list in early summer before the tall Asiatic lilies came into month-long bloom in July.

Williamsburg was in the perfect climate zone for bulb

plants, and he had dreamed these lush additions to his garden for far too long to stay his imagination. It was *his* garden after all, Hooper decided. It did not belong to the squirrels. He decided he would definitely not have his desires thwarted by marauders. Hooper would just spend more time in the garden and run them off with thrown pebbles and shouts. His wife, Mae, said she would help when she could find the time.

Dr. Lear drove his SUV to the garden center in Williamsburg to begin his first major planting of bulbs. He was filled with excitement and anticipation. He did not, however, anticipate that this was the day he would meet someone new to his life as a gardener. And new to the life of his garden.

After careful study, Hooper had concluded that Van Engelen, in Bantam, Connecticut, was the finest source of bulbs in the world. Other local gardeners, including Hooper's friends who worked at the garden center, agreed.

Van Engelen sold only in bulk, and the prices were best when fifty or a hundred bulbs of a single variety were ordered. In some instances, such as with the beautiful blue scilla known as Siberian squill, a hundred bulbs was the minimum order allowed. To assure they were receiving the highest quality and largest variety of bulbs available, a few local gardeners had loosely organized a sizable order and would divide the varieties among themselves. Some would trade the bulbs further among gardeners in their neighborhoods and families.

The order of bulbs from Van Engelen had come in the day before. Hooper was excited to be taking his garden in a new and lush direction, despite his ongoing quarrel with the thieving bushy-tailed tree rats other people called squirrels. Of the two thousand bulbs in the order, twelve hundred were his. To

Hooper, the assortment represented the future. He loaded the Van Engelen boxes into the back of his SUV. Although they were half empty, he couldn't move the bulbs from one cardboard box to another because the names of the varieties had been scrawled on the outsides. Some of the individual packages of bulbs had been opened and used by others in the group.

After the boxes were loaded, Hooper found a bag of bone meal and added two large bags of a neutral-pH planting soil mixed with aged leaf compost. And then he was on his way. He drove carefully, peering at oncoming traffic through his new bifocals, tilting his head slightly to bring bits of the outside world into sharper focus.

Hooper saw three squirrels hopping about in his front yard as he backed the SUV into the driveway and then inside his garage. He would store most of the bulbs, the ones he couldn't get to right way, in the refrigerator in the garage, keeping them fresh and hungry for warm, soft soil. He tumbled out of the vehicle as happy as a schoolboy.

When he opened the back of the vehicle, he found two light green eyes looking at him from inside one of the boxes of bulbs.

"Hello there," Hooper said.

The yellow cat lifted her head from the box, staring not so much at Hooper as somewhere beyond, as if listening to the call of a bird in the distance.

"Where did you come from?"

Hooper saw a flash of nose and whiskers. In an instant, the cat was out of the box, out of the SUV, and out of the garage. He followed the cat around the side of his house. He pushed up his glasses with one finger and watched the sleek yellow cat go over the garden fence in a single movement.

The cat was in the garden.

"Hey, cat!"

Hooper opened the gate and breathed in the airy fragrance of the last blooms of the doubled pink Stanwell perpetual roses that covered sixteen feet of lattice on the inside of his garden fence. He walked well into the acre of garden and discovered the cat was sitting on the stone bench by the koi pond. She must have been drawn by the sound of water. Now, her tail twitched. Her four legs cocked. She was watching something with great intensity, ignoring Hooper's approach.

A squirrel hopped across the wide path in front of the arbor, its fluffy tail flagging up and down. It paused, chattered, then hopped again. The cat was off the bench in a second, rushing the squirrel at full speed, chasing it across the rock garden and up a small decorative redbud. Two sparrows flew quickly from the tree. The limber branches bounced and waved as the cat shot up the tree as quickly as the squirrel in front of her.

Soon, the squirrel had run to the narrow end of a redbud branch and turned to face the yellow cat. Undeterred, and in perfect balance on the limb, the cat came quickly after the squirrel. To Hooper's amazement, the squirrel, trying to back up further, lost purchase and fell to the ground with a thud. Two heart-shaped leaves torn from the tree floated down after it.

The squirrel seemed stunned in the grass, but only for a moment. It righted itself and sped to the nearest edge of the garden. In fear for its life, it raced up the fence and leapt into the neighbor's yard. The yellow cat lazed on her perch above.

Although he had much to do first, and though proper introductions were in order, Hooper knew at that very moment he had made a valuable acquaintance. He kept his fingers crossed, went inside the house, and called the garden center. The collarless yellow cat, he learned, was a stray. She had been pestering people at the garden center for the past few days, playing among the plants, drinking from the water pail.

"We have a cat," he told his wife.

Hooper ran a quick series of errands and came home with a cat carrier, a litter box, litter, feeding and water dishes, and four brands of cat food.

Mae rushed out the front door as Hooper pulled into the driveway.

"Just horrid," she told him. "It was just horrid!"

What could have happened? Had one of their kids called with a problem? Hillary was pregnant, and there had been problems with her first delivery, although all had turned out well.

"The cat . . . ," Mae sputtered, pointing in the general direction of the garden. "That cat! It killed a squirrel, Hooper! It was just horrid. All the screeching, and the other squirrels in the trees and on the fence were chattering like monkeys. They were screaming at the cat, Hooper, I swear."

"Calm down, darling. It's okay."

"It's not okay. Listen to me, there is a dead squirrel in the yard, and that cat . . . that cat refuses to leave. He just sits on the stone bench like it's his now."

"Hers," Hooper corrected. "It's *her* bench now."

"But it was bloody murder, Hoop! You aren't listening to me!"

Not listening to Mae twenty-four hours a day was part of the reason the retired dentist had started gardening in the first place. Of course, he didn't say so.

"It can't . . . it cannot, absolutely *cannot* happen again! Do you hear me? I will go out of my mind if I ever have to see or hear a squirrel being murdered again."

"It likely won't," Hooper said nonchalantly. He handed Mae the cat carrier from the backseat. "The other squirrels were watching, you see. They know now. Cleo's yard is off-limits. Strictly off-limits to squirrels from this day on."

"Cleo?"

"Short for Cleome, our cat. Did you see the whiskers on her? They look just like *Cleome hassleriana*."

"Not *our* cat," Mae said. "*Your* cat. She's your cat. I don't want anything to do with squirrel killers. Not a single thing."

"Let's just hope she likes some of this food."

Hooper unloaded the rest of his purchases. He called the veterinarian, who told him to bring the new cat in anytime. The vet was always pleased to work with newly adopted strays.

It took Hooper three days of placing food inside the open cat carrier that he set in the garden each morning before Cleo would approach her food while he was present. That afternoon, he placed a small toy laced with catnip in the cat carrier. Soon, they were on their way to the vet's.

Hooper explained everything to the yellow cat during the drive.

"You have a home, Cleo, for as long as you like. It's yours. The garden and the house. You'll love the plants. And the pond. Of course, you are already fond of that, aren't you? Be careful with Mae for a bit, but she'll come around. You'll see."

She didn't seem to mind being in the cat carrier. She liked being in boxes, after all. The carrier was her space to occupy, and she knew it instantly, just as she knew the garden would be her forever home. Cats prefer to live in one place their entire lives and to make it their territory. Cleo was no exception.

Cleo was spayed, treated for ear mites, bathed, vaccinated. Tagged and collared.

"You have a valuable cat," the vet informed Hooper. "Usually, only feral cats will take on a squirrel. Cleo here is lithe and strong. She is young and ready to have a home. She'll bond quickly, with just a little kindness."

"She'll get plenty of attention. I spend all day in the garden, and she seems to like it there."

"Start by scratching the top of her head between her ears, then a little on down the back of her neck. Don't touch her tail, and you'll be rubbing her entire back in no time. Oh, a little gentle stroking under the chin goes a long way with cats."

Hooper nodded.

"Find a place she likes to be and quietly occupy that space with her. She'll get used to you quickly. When she starts bunting, she'll be your cat."

"Bunting?"

The veterinarian grinned. "She'll rub her head on you when she has the opportunity. She'll bunt her head on your hands and your arms, on your legs. This is how cats scent the people they own. She'll strive to keep her scent on you, so other animals will know you're taken."

Hooper laughed. "That I am, doctor." He pushed his glasses back into place. "That I am."

The bulbs took to the blessings of nature in Hooper's

garden over the years. Many became naturalized. Cleo created secret cat trails through the flower beds, and hid when she felt like hiding under dropping leaves and the blossoms of her favorite plants. Cleo always started her morning by lying stretched out in the sun in the middle of the garden, where she could be seen by the squirrels, if any of them were wondering whether or not the coast was clear yet. It wasn't.

Hooper started his days for the next several years by sitting on the stone bench, watching the brightly colored koi swimming in suspended motion and then darting under the shade of the watercress, which drifted away from the current. Cleo watched with him. It was her bench, after all. Her whiskers and eyebrows twitched when one of the smaller fish darted by.

Sometimes, the two of them talked. Sometimes, they didn't say a word and simply listened to the moving water in the pond, to the morning songs of birds carried on the breeze.

When it was time to feed the koi, Cleo was particularly enthralled to see the brightly colored fish lift their heads from the water, their mouths open and moving, as if to speak. The fish had whiskers, just like she did. Cleo moved her mouth, flexing her own whiskers, as if lip reading what the fish might have to say. She understood somehow that she and Hooper were the caretakers of the spotted underwater wildlife and never once troubled a single koi by batting the water with her paw. Well, not that Hooper was aware of, anyway.

No matter how early Mae got up in the morning, she would see Hooper and Cleo from the windows of the house, already in the garden. Early sunlight reflected from the lenses of his glasses as he looked at every plant, said hello to every fish. Cleo's head moved with his, seeing what he saw. Even in the coldest weather, he sat with his first cup of coffee on the bench beside the pond.

As Hooper aged and his time grew near, he talked to Mae often about seeing heaven.

"Heaven is a garden, I bet," he said. "And everything is in bloom in heaven. Heaven is a garden and a cat."

Hooper was in his eighties when he fell in the garden from a stroke and hit his head. He lay in his hospital bed for about a week, unconscious but at peaceful rest, until he passed away.

The night before the funeral, Mae looked high and low for Hooper's glasses. They hadn't taken them to the hospital. Hooper, she knew, needed his glasses. If he were buried without his glasses, he wouldn't be able to see much of heaven at all. She couldn't find them anywhere. She looked on every surface in the house, in every drawer, under every piece of furniture.

Hillary spent the week at her mother's house. Her youngest, just sixteen now, stayed, too, wondering out loud if she was too chubby to ever be loved by anyone who was really cool. Three generations of women searched the house for Grandpa's glasses, to no avail.

Mae couldn't sleep. As early as the sun came up, she was peering out the windows, pacing. Thinking of a new place Hooper's glasses might be, she flung the cushions from the couch. No glasses there.

Cleo walked silently into the room and watched her.

"What are you looking at?" Mae wanted to know.

The tall yellow cat twitched her whiskers, studying the situation.

"Help me find his glasses," Mae pleaded with the cat.

"Won't you help?"

Cleo walked into the kitchen, twitching her tail.

"It's time for breakfast, isn't it?" Mae said. "Oh, all right then."

She followed Cleo into the kitchen. But instead of waiting to be fed, Cleo walked purposefully to the sliding glass door that led into the garden.

"Well, go outside then and look for his glasses." Mae let the cat out.

She continued wandering through the rooms of the house, trying to think of anyplace she hadn't already looked twice for Hooper's glasses.

From an upstairs window, she saw Hooper in the garden. She stopped in her tracks. She stared out the window as hard as an old woman can stare.

Hooper stood by the Japanese maple. He looked so peaceful that Mae smiled to see him standing there. He even winked at her. She saw him wink! When he winked, Mae realized he wasn't wearing his glasses, and the peaceful feeling evaporated into empty air. She hurried back downstairs to look more closely at the garden, to find the red-leafed maple, the bench, to see if Hooper was really there.

Cleo was at the glass door, reaching both paws high above her head and letting them slide down the glass. She left muddy streaks.

"Damn cat," Mae muttered. She slid the door open to let Cleo back into the house. The yellow cat was soaking wet. She looked skinny and harmless and pathetic. Cleo sat just inside the glass door. She licked a front paw carefully. She licked the other one.

It was not raining. The hoses hadn't been turned on. The sprinklers were quiet.

"You've been in the pond," Mae said. "There'll be no more of that, young lady!"

Mae retrieved a tea towel from the kitchen, then stopped. *The pond!* She rushed outdoors. A very wet Cleo followed her out, then quickly took the lead, eagerly showing Mae the way along the pebbled path to the koi pond. Cleo strode to a particular spot at the pond's edge and sat on her hind legs, watching the water, her whiskers pointed forward.

Peering through the circulating water, looking beyond the brightly colored koi, Mae saw them at last. Her heart leapt. Hooper's glasses were in the pond. It was where he fell when he had his stroke. Right where Cleo was sitting.

Mae fished them out of the pond and hurried into the house with her critical prize. Hooper would see heaven now. She rinsed and dried off the glasses with care, polishing the thick lenses. She'd have Hillary take them to the funeral home.

Excited to tell the first one up that she had found Hooper's glasses, Mae showed them to her sixteen-year-old sleepy-eyed granddaughter.

"Where were they, Grandma?"

"In the pond." Mae smiled triumphantly. "They were in the pond. But I didn't find them, Cleo did."

"Cleo?"

"Our cat, dear. Lordy, she was wet. She'd been in the pond. We went outside together, and she took me right to them. And there they were. Isn't that something?"

"Yes . . . yes, it is," the teenager stammered. "Cleo's been dead for two years now, Grandma. She's buried by the ruffled daffodils out back. Don't you remember?"

Mae touched a finger to her upper lip. When she checked the sliding door for muddy paw streaks, the glass was as clean as a whisker on a cat.

Rose Perfume

≈ ≈ ≈ ≈ ≈ ≈ ≈ ≈ ≈ ≈ ≈ ≈ ≈ ≈

A seventeenth-century Spanish fort still stands on the Atlantic coast of Florida. The well-preserved Castillo de San Marcos, located in a twenty-five-acre park in St. Augustine, holds a place in the earliest colonial history of America. The original stonework of the national monument also holds the story of two lovers and a cat.

Their story is carried on the air as the scent of rose perfume, a perfume that cannot be covered by stone.

The rose perfume masks a deeper, sickly odor.

While the fort was undergoing expansion in the 1740s, a Spanish war galleon sailed through the St. Augustine inlet with a cat on board, carried in the arms of a young military bride. The small domestic pet was destined to become the oldest known cat ghost in the American South.

50 Rose Perfume

The feline walks the grounds of the historic Castillo de San Marcos on silent paws yet today. A sighting of the cat is always accompanied by the smell of rose perfume. Throughout the South, the "San Marcos Cat" has become known as a ghost of eternal love.

Visitors who have seen the creature say the cat is gray. But it may be that only the ghost of the cat is gray. Old ghosts sometimes fade in color over the centuries. All witnesses note, though, that the cat wears a shiny silver collar. Most visitors never see the cat at all, but many have been surprised by the scent of rose perfume at one turn or another among the walls of coquina shells and stone.

History does not record the name of the cat attached to the painful demise of two lovers who found themselves doomed to die slowly within the impenetrable walls of the Castillo de San Marcos.

Only the cat could keep them alive.

Only the cat could bring them death.

The Spanish began construction of the Castillo de San Marcos in 1672, when St. Augustine was at the edge of the known world. A far-outlying bastion of the largest empire ever created, the fort was constructed to protect and defend Spain's claims in the New World. Though caught in the whirlwind of early colonial warfare between Spain and Britain, the fort itself was never defeated in battle. Outside, its scarred walls still stand witness to bombardment and battle. Inside, the stone walls of one room witnessed a smaller story on the world's stage, a story of undying human love and the devotion of a small domestic cat to her human mistress.

When the structure underwent refortification in the

1740s, the interior rooms were extended into the courtyard to make them deeper. Vaulted ceilings replaced the wooden roof. The coquina-and-stone ceilings also made it possible to mount heavy Spanish cannons around the perimeter of the gun deck, rather than just in the corner bastions, as in the original design.

The construction was overseen by a Spanish colonel who sailed to the Americas with his young bride and an entourage of attendants and servants. Colonel Luis Gaspar was an aging favorite of the Spanish throne. His marriage to the young and spirited Marianna was his third. The young girl was given in marriage by her father in an arrangement for anticipated political favors.

Luis Gaspar had little time for his wife. The stern military commander had nothing to say to her. Women didn't understand the world, especially a woman as young as Marianna. She was mere decoration for the colonel, a bright and golden ornament for formal occasions. She was another badge he'd won from the throne.

Marianna blossomed in the New World and soon found herself wildly attracted to the more youthful Miguel Antonio, a captain newly assigned to the garrison at St. Augustine. The young captain in turn fell helplessly in love with the married woman. Theirs was a love that was doomed from the beginning. But it was also a love that neither could end.

Marianna wore a richly scented rose perfume to mask the odor of the physical love she shared in secret with Miguel. She had the perfume formulated by the garrison pharmacy. The doctor was sympathetic to Marianna's plight. It was only natural for a young woman to fall in love with a man close to her own age, with a man who adored her. Soon, the couple would learn that Marianna was the property of a cruel master.

When the illicit love came to the attention of Colonel Gaspar, the punishment was swift and severe. A ruined woman now, Marianna was locked inside an interior stone room and chained to the wall. A heavy wooden door sealed her fate. The door was cut with a small window, over which were bolted iron bars.

The next day, Miguel Antonio was stripped of his rank, the buttons cut from his uniform. Marianna's sentence was death. Miguel's was different, though just as cruel. By command of the colonel, he was taken to the room under armed guard and locked inside with Marianna. He, too, was left in chains but was given the option of release if he would publicly denounce his love of the colonel's wife. He would be returned to Spain and put in prison there, but he would be alive.

No food or water was provided the lovers in their stone cell.

Upon hearing the harsh sentences, the doctor in the pharmacy went at once to Marianna's rooms and retrieved the pet cat she'd brought with her from Spain. He carefully clasped a small vial to the cat's collar and filled it with water. The human body can survive much longer without food than without water.

The doctor brought the cat to the outer room. She knew instantly where her mistress lay behind the locked door. While he spoke briefly to the guard about a salve he'd brought for the guard to try on his itching feet, the cat hurried across the floor and leapt through the window in the cell door.

Later that day, the cat returned to the pharmacy. A small

note had been rolled into the vial. Written with a pencil from Marianna's chatelaine were the simple words, "*Gracias, por favor más*"—"Thank you, more please."

The cat was sent to the dungeon time and time again, through the day and through the night.

It is unknown, of course, how the lovers spent their time, of what they spoke and what they did not dare to speak. Miguel Antonio refused each morning and each evening to be released from death, to be released from Marianna's fate, a fate that was soon to be his own. Small amounts of water from a vial would not prevent death, only delay it.

On the fourth day, the doctor found another note rolled into the cat's vial. It read, "*Veneno, por favor*"—"Poison, please."

The doctor did as Marianna so plainly requested. He formulated an oral poison that would be fatal with a mere touch of the tongue. Its smell was strong and offensive. He scented the black liquid with rose perfume, hoping to mask the repulsive odor. The faithful cat, Marianna's pet since her arrival in St. Augustine, performed her duty.

As an act of love, Miguel Antonio sipped the poison first, so Marianna would not fear that she might die alone. A touch to parched lips, a touch upon the tongue, and the lovers died locked in one last kiss. Their hearts beat as one, then together beat no more. Miguel and Marianna died with their eyes closed to a rose-scented kiss.

A few years ago, a portion of the Castillo de San Marcos was closed to the public. One of the heavy cannons fell through the roof of the structure. Workers were called in to reinforce the original ceilings against further collapse. Those who entered the chamber quickly noticed a rich, sweet rose odor coming from a sealed-off room adjacent to where the cannon had fallen. The perfume had been sealed within for two centuries. Inside the previously hidden room, they discovered two skeletons. One was that of a man, the other, a woman.

Tour guides routinely tell visitors the story behind the corpses, how the wife of one of the Spanish commanders was caught by her husband having an affair with a lesser officer, and how in punishment of her infidelity the lovers were sealed into the small room and left to die without food or water.

Not entirely without water, though.

The room is now open to the public.

Some visitors still smell a faint rose perfume when touring the grounds of the fortress. Many report seeing a small cat with a bright silver collar about the grounds, most often in the area of the recently discovered room. The cat cannot be followed. She simply disappears around a corner.

The San Marcos Cat may have faded in color through the years. The scent of rose perfume has faded as well. The perfume is for now a faint and airy memory of a bygone love and of the faithful cat that brought fate-scarred lovers life when they required it.

The same faithful cat, now a ghost, carried to her mistress a final drink when life, but not love, was brought to its end.

A Piece of Yarn

≈ ≈ ≈ ≈ ≈ ≈ ≈ ≈ ≈ ≈ ≈ ≈ ≈ ≈ ≈

They say that Jackson, Mississippi, has as many lawyers as cats. And the cats are smarter.

Attorney L. Anson Emery stared at a badly misshapen wool sweater left for him as a birthday gift by none other than William Barkeley, Jr., one of the wealthiest men in Jackson when he died, and Anson's second uncle by marriage. The old codger's remembering Anson's birthday was good. The sweater was bad. It was of thick knitted stripes in black and yellow. Anson could barely stand to think of it, that crazy old man knitting alone all day and all night in his mansion just off Belhaven Street.

Nobody wears wool in Jackson. The climate is molten at best. The city is built on an extinct volcano, and most people believe the Jackson heat comes up through the soil. The humidity is Mississippi's own contribution to the city in America that feels most like living in an oven. Summers in Jackson are so hot and humid that they make the inside of your mouth sweat.

Jackson is one of the few cities in America where in August you can sit outside and watch trees melt. There are no sea breezes of an evening, unlike Galveston, Mobile, and Biloxi. The only change in weather in Jackson comes when overheated thunderstorms drop buckets of rain on the ground. It's so hot the wind can't blow. Wind comes only in the form of tornadoes.

The heat drives people bonkers in Jackson. And humidity keeps them from doing anything about it.

Anson should know. His uncle went nuts. There was nothing more to be said than that. Anson worried that the rich old coot had given all his money to a television evangelist or to that so-called nurse he had paid to be there every day and cook him lunch and supper. The old man had lived his last years alone, except for that nurse's coming by. And except for the cat.

When Anson had driven by the stately house at night, it always looked as if it were lit up for Christmas. Every light had been on every night.

He looked at the sweater again. It wasn't anywhere near his birthday. But that's what his richest relative had left him when he died, that and the care of his cat.

Anson had inherited a hand-knit sweater, along with a scrawled note that read, "Happy Birthday, Anson." The cat got the rest of the estate.

In 1839, Mississippi had become the first state to allow married women to possess and administer their own property.

The law was enacted in Jackson. It didn't say anything about cats owning property.

But laws of inheritance hadn't stopped his uncle. The old man created a caretaker's trust that tied all his personal property and wealth, including the Belhaven mansion, to the care of the cat. The cat, according to the legal paperwork, would remain in her home forever, and it was the charge of the executor to see that she was happy there and without want of any kind. The estate was eight million dollars in trust and a mansion full of priceless antiques.

As executor of Uncle William's estate, Anson vowed to see what he could do about that.

He dropped by the mansion, fired the nurse when she arrived, and killed the cat.

Anson wrote "Natural Causes" on the appropriate paperwork at his uncle's downtown law firm. *Death by lawyer*, he thought, was *natural causes*. He laughed out loud.

Anson specialized in D.U.I.'s and divorces in his own legal practice and didn't understand the complicated twists and turns of wills and trusts. His uncle's personal attorney explained matters simply enough.

"You're looking at years before final control of the property and access to the money will be free for your inheritance," the white-haired lawyer told him. "I'm afraid your uncle's trust doesn't provide for a quick and easy route to remove the assets of the estate from the trust upon the death of the cat. The trust stays in place until five years after the cat's natural death. Did you not understand that?"

"I see," Anson said blankly. Of course, he hadn't understood that. At least he'd gotten a small head start by killing the cat.

"And everything goes probate at that point. Probate is slow as molasses. Two more years, maybe three. Until then, as executor, you will receive a monthly stipend. It's the same as if the cat were alive. And of course, you can draw expenses for maintenance of the house. It cannot be sold or rented out, and the terms of the trust name you as sole occupant of the property. No one else may spend the night there."

"You mean I have to stay there?"

"Yes, young man, in order to draw the stipend, you do."

"Oh."

Since the stipend was a measly ten thousand dollars a month, the legal limit of the trust, the bulk of his uncle's money—of Anson's money—would sit idle for what seemed like forever. Five years was forever when you were waiting on money. Five years of long, hot days in Jackson, Mississippi.

Anson decided he would find a way to break the five-year extension of his uncle's trust, even if he had to go back to law school and read every state inheritance law ever written.

Anson's first night in the mansion was not a happy one. He didn't like being there alone.

He discovered an unopened bottle of twelve-year-old single malt Scotch in his uncle's cabinet. He carried it with him, taking a sip as he felt like it. He walked through the house to survey what antiques might be sold. Anson peered out through the stained-glass window on the landing but saw only the reflection of his own face. It scared him. For a sudden moment, he thought someone was watching him, and his heart leapt.

Safely tucked in bed in one of the large upstairs guest rooms, Anson wondered what the weather in France was like in the summer. He had enough money to live on a yacht anywhere in the world, if he could just get his hands on it. Maybe he would fly a few places and see what was what. Anson counted places like sheep, Rio, Paris, Cannes. . . .

He was bothered in his sleep. Something light and feathery constantly crossed Anson's face. He dreamed his face was inside a spider web.

When Anson woke in the morning, the spider web was gone. He found a piece of yarn at the foot of the bed and another small piece by his pillow. He noticed an indentation in the pillow beside his. It looked as if something the size of a head had been sitting there.

Forget it, he thought. He must have moved around in his sleep.

Pieces of yarn were all over the house.

Next time, he'd try the fifteen-year-old Scotch. No reason to save it for a special occasion. Having a better night's sleep was occasion enough.

He carried out box after box of the old man's antiques, small things he thought would readily sell, one or two at a time to every antique shop in town. Ceramic vases, silver candlesticks, bronzes, daguerreotypes. He even managed to wedge two framed oil paintings between the front and back seats of his red Mercedes-Benz.

Some of his uncle's family things were worth a lot, he learned.

Anson sold a Newcomb College vase to an antique dealer for two thousand dollars cash. In the glaze was a picture of a moss-draped tree in moonlight. The bottom was signed. The dealer called Anson later that day to ask if he had more. He told the young attorney that he had already placed the vase with a valued customer. He also told Anson in passing that a piece of yarn was found inside the vase.

Why wouldn't there be? Anson thought. The entire house was full of yarn. Balls and packages of yarn were everywhere and in every color. Yarn overflowed large paper sacks in every corner of every room. It was driving him crazy. Pieces of yarn clung to his clothes. Yarn seemed to follow him around the old man's house. Wherever he went, there was yarn.

Every morning, he woke up and briefly felt as if he couldn't move. Yarn would be there with him, pieces of it on the bed, on the floor next to the bed. Some of it was tied in little knots. Anson didn't know much about knitting but thought it was something along the lines of tying knots over and over again. If he didn't know better, he would have thought his uncle had come back from the grave in the middle of the night and thrown pieces of yarn at him. Anson found them in the morning, in loosening wads on the bed by his feet and wrists.

His uncle's Scotch ran out. Anson switched to bourbon.

The night he brought home the yacht brochures, he woke up in bed from a dream that he was drowning in a calm ocean and that someone had tied a weight to his chest. When he opened his eyes, he saw the cat sitting right on top of him. A piece of yellow yarn was in her mouth.

Anson was too startled to speak. For the life of him, as much as he wanted to, he couldn't move. The cat that Anson had killed blinked at him and then was gone. Finally, he was able to throw back the covers and get out of bed. He paced the room. Cats can see in the dark, he knew. The cat could see Anson just fine.

He phoned the paralegal.

"Yes, I know what time it is," Anson said. "You're on twenty-four-hour call, remember?"

He waited for the employee to clear his throat.

"Grab a pad and write this down. Is there some sort of condition where a person wakes up but isn't really awake? And they are unable to move? Call me back on that."

Eight minutes later, the phone rang. The paralegal was a whiz at research.

"It's called 'the hag phenomenon,' " he said. "According to the Internet, it's a condition of sleep when you wake too quickly, where you feel utterly paralyzed, as if you're being held down and can't move. It comes with age. And whatever you were dreaming, well, you still see a little bit of that, but you think you are entirely awake."

"You see what you're dreaming?" Anson said. "Not what's really there?"

"I wouldn't worry about it. Try drinking a little less late at night. And turn the air conditioning down. That recirculated air messes with your head."

"Yeah, sure. I'll turn the air conditioning down when I'm in France. I wonder if they have air conditioning in Tahiti."

"Don't ask," the paralegal said, and clicked off his phone.

Anson went back to sleep. He had the same dream again. He tried to swim but couldn't move his arms or legs. The ocean was on top of him, and all he could do was stare up at it. Fish swam by. They all had whiskers and looked like they wanted to eat him. Their teeth were little shiny knives and forks. They were waiting for Anson to drown.

He struggled to push himself from the depths of sleep. He

woke with a start, his eyes wide open. His bed was covered with cats. Cats of different sizes and different colors. They were right on top of him. They were at the corners of the bed. The dead cat was right in the middle of them. For a minute, Anson couldn't move. He was filled with dread. And fear.

The bed may as well have been on fire. He couldn't do a thing about it.

Finally, he was able to scream. He flailed his arms at the cats, drawing his legs up in one quick motion. The cats leapt off the bed and disappeared.

Downstairs, he opened a bottle of vodka. It would have to do. The old man's bar had been reduced to little else. It was three in the morning. He'd been asleep only a half-hour since calling the paralegal.

Anson climbed the stairs in his underwear, drinking. He turned off the air conditioning.

"There's no hag," he said out loud to no one. "It's just a cat."

Never kill a cat if you want to sleep at night.

Anson convinced himself he was not insane. It was the barometer. A thunderstorm must be coming. He was under a lot of pressure, that was all. A lot of pressure, and too much air conditioning.

He wasn't a little boy anymore. There was nothing to be afraid of in the dark. He was an adult and could go back to bed anytime he wanted to.

Anson didn't show up for an appointment at his uncle's law firm. In fact, he hadn't been heard from in several days when the Jackson police broke down the door of the Belhaven mansion. His car was in the driveway. Inside the house, the lights were on in every room. The air conditioning was off, and the house had been closed up tight. It was like an oven in there.

Only it smelled worse.

Anson's death turned into a rather sensational murder case, as yet unsolved. The state investigators released few details. They kept their reports under lock and key. They considered it important and confidential evidence that Anson's hands were tied to the bed by loosely braided lengths of yarn. Only the murderer and the police knew that his ankles were tied to the footboard posts in a similar fashion, and that Anson was strangled in his bed by a curiously woven noose of knitting yarn in a strange variety of colors.

Anson died with his eyes wide open, the pathologist said.

Evidence specialists determined that the small pieces of yarn weren't cut by scissors or knives. Rather, the ends appeared to have been chewed and bitten off by someone. The loose weaving of the yarn pieces was errant and disorganized, the end result misshapen but still strong enough for the job.

A few weeks later, the antique dealer in Jackson bought back the Newcomb College vase Anson had sold him, this time for only a thousand dollars because the widow didn't care to dicker. The original customer, her husband, had died coughing in his sleep. He'd apparently been chewing on a piece of yarn, and it got balled up at the back of his throat, she said.

The estate of William Barkeley, Jr., was settled without a will this time. The contents of his mansion were sold at auction at the request of an attorney from his law firm. The attorney lives in the house now. He has two cats in the yard.

They say Jackson, Mississippi, has more lawyers than cats. And that's no yarn.

Some people say Jackson has more antiques than either lawyers or cats. People travel from around the word to buy antiques there. It is likely they'll find small pieces of yarn hidden inside some of them.

It's something to chew on.

The Lightning Tree

≈ ≈ ≈ ≈ ≈ ≈ ≈ ≈ ≈ ≈ ≈ ≈ ≈ ≈ ≈ ≈

Baton Rouge was where early French explorers found a red pole stuck in the ground.

Sieur d'Iberville and a group of two hundred men came up the Mississippi River from New Orleans in 1699. On March 17, the exploration party discovered the first bluff on the river. A potential town site free from the threat of flood, the bluff was quickly charted and investigated. The red cypress pole, upon which were mounted severed animal heads, was recognized as a boundary marker.

The French guessed incorrectly when they decided the pole of heads marked a hunting boundary between Native American tribes. Tribal boundaries required no such demarcation. Some say the blood-smeared baton did not mark the limits of

a culture's domain. It marked the limits of human safety.

The pole was a warning. The bluff above the river, legend has it, was a place where witches were killed.

The heads were those of witches who had taken on the souls of woodland creatures. Witches were driven to the bluff and slain. Upon death, their bodies reverted to the wild animals they had become. Their human faces became the furred faces of animals. American Indians often took on the spirits of animals for battle. This was a common religious practice. Native American witches, however, took on the spirits of animals for convenience, for easy travel, for play, and for mayhem.

A man who changed souls with a crow could travel great distances and return in a single day. A man who changed souls with a bat could overhear conversations whispered in the dark of night. A man who changed souls with a Louisiana panther could kill another person and not be suspected of the crime.

The kitchen witchcraft of the Cajun and Creole populations, a witchcraft of potions and charms, formed an interesting mix with the Native American culture around Baton Rouge. It was an area where the swamp magic of graveyard spells met the animal magic of a dying Native American culture.

Witches in Louisiana have been changing places with cats for hundreds of years.

People traveling Highway 190 between Baton Rouge and Livonia sometimes see a flash of lightning late at night in a field north of the highway, even when the weather is clear. The lightning illuminates a large, old tree in the distance. In fact, the flash of hot, brilliant light seems to originate in the tree. The locals call this "the Lightning Tree." Like other ghostly

69

lights in the South, it has never been scientifically explained. Its branches have been burned, but the tree survives.

No one is quite sure how long lightning has been flashing on and off in that tree. But it's been years now. Few people who see the tree momentarily light up at night associate the phenomenon with witchcraft. Witches in Louisiana are associated with other things.

"My grandfather said that witches will change you into a horse while you're sleeping and ride you places at night," a boy named Ralph proclaimed one day. "That's how they get around in a hurry when they want to."

"Your grandfather is nuts," fourteen-year-old Charley Hammond said.

"Is not," Ralph said.

"Ever time you lie, I get to punch you in the arm. You're still thirteen, and I'm not. I can punch you in the arm anytime I want."

"Okay, he's nuts," Ralph said quickly. "But you've been fourteen for only two days, so shut up."

Ralph lived in the house up the road. He was in the same class as Charley, and they rode the school bus together. Charley Hammond turned fourteen the year lightning first struck that tree north of Highway 190. Charley saw it happen. So did Ralph.

For Charley's birthday, he and Ralph were allowed to have a sleepover at the Hammond house. Charley wanted to camp out in the attic. His mother said it was okay, but they had to be quiet up there. The old house had crossbeams in the attic to support the rafters. It was just like a fort, with one small window at each end.

If Charley had a tent, the boys would have used it in the attic. Instead, they spread out pallets on the floor. They used a big flashlight for a campfire and ate Vienna sausages right out of the can. After telling stories almost all night, Ralph mentioned Alice Webster. She was the most beautiful girl in junior high, and they had to say her name out loud before going to sleep.

"She takes her top off to wash her hair," Ralph said.

"How do you know that?" Charley sat up. "I'm going to punch you if you're lying."

"Because my sister does. I'm not allowed in the kitchen when she's washing her hair, but I saw her once."

Charley lay back down. He didn't have to punch Ralph.

"My sister washes her hair in her bra," Ralph said. "Alice Webster does too, I bet."

Charley Hammond was fourteen now and allowed to know things like this about Alice. He thought about it awhile, then fell asleep.

Late into the night, a clap of thunder woke them. It was right on top of the house. It sounded like a cannon. Rain pummeled the roof. A flash of lightning lit up the attic windows. It was like someone was taking their picture. They found their flashlights and turned them on. They pointed them at each other, then across the attic floor to the window.

"It's going to leak," Ralph said. He pointed his flashlight straight up.

"Is not," Charley said, but he looked up anyway.

Both teenagers froze in mid-breath. A woman in a white dress sat scrunched over on the crossbeam above them. She was dripping wet. Her hair hung on either side of her face. It was soaked with rain. Her eyes glowed in the flashlight beams. She stared down at the boys, turning her head from one side to the other, studying each of them in turn.

"Hello, boys," she said. "Sure is a bad night for being out."

Charley dropped his flashlight. He barely noticed.

"You're the Hammond boy," the woman said to Charley. "I know where I am, you see."

Both boys stared with their mouths open.

The woman looked at Ralph. He began to shake.

"And I know you, too. Your mother is active in the church. I've seen her there on Wednesdays and Saturdays both."

Charley tired to swallow without closing his mouth. He made a clucking noise at the back of his throat.

The woman wrung her hair in her hands. Water poured down on the pallets. Both boys drew their legs up.

"Guess I better go, if you got nothing to say to me. Now, don't you boys be telling anyone you saw me tonight, you hear?" They nodded slowly, mouths still open.

The woman in white dropped from the beam. When she landed at the end of their pallets, she was a white cat with a long white tail. The cat ran to the window at one end of the attic. There was another crash of thunder. The cat turned its head to look back at the boys. Then it leapt into the stormy night. It leapt through the window as if it could fly.

Ralph's flashlight fell.

"That window is closed shut," Charley said.

Ralph didn't reply. He had the edge of his blanket in his mouth.

"It was just a cat," Charley said. "The whole time, it was just a cat. Did you hear it talk?"

The other boy was quiet.

"Ralph, did you hear it talk?"

"No," Ralph said around the edges of the blanket he held in his teeth.

"She said she knew who you are." A sheet of heavy rain pounded the roof. "Hey, do you smell that? It smells like pee!"

Ralph didn't say a thing. He wasn't going to let a witch know who he was, if he could help it. He'd grow a mustache as soon as he could. He'd buy sunglasses and a hat to wear until then.

Charley found his flashlight and walked across the floor of their attic fort to the window. Ralph wrapped himself in his blanket and followed. Charley touched the window. It was closed tight. Thunder and lightning came together in a single loud, crackling crash. A bright flash illuminated the sky above the big tree by the fence. Both boys jerked back from the window. They felt as if they'd been hit.

In the sudden lightning, they saw a woman flying over the tree. She was dressed in white. It was not a cat. Cats can't fly. Witches can.

A shower of sparks burst from the top of the tree, then all the light went out. A branch fell to the ground with the rain. It sounded like the earth had been cracked. The image of the woman at the top of the tree was etched in their memories as the two teenagers continued to stare.

"Did you see that?" Charley asked.

"No," Ralph said.

Charley turned around and hit him in the arm, just below the shoulder.

"I guess you saw something. You peed your pants."

It wasn't much fun, being a witch caught in a Louisiana thunderstorm at night. Lightning struck at things flying in the air. She'd been about to land in that tree when the lightning hit. It hurt. The clap of thunder drowned out her scream. The witch was damaged, her hair singed. Her lips were hot to the touch of a fingertip. She didn't know if she could fly. She wasn't sure she ever really wanted to again. She could run around on cat feet and be just fine. And she could climb just about anything.

She could climb about anything but down from that tree, the witch discovered. Every time she touched so much as a toe to the ground, electricity shot up her leg amid a bright flash of light. She quickly drew her leg back and rubbed it for comfort. She tried again, with the same result. Ouch, that hurt! And again.

If I try one more time, she thought, *I'll surely catch fire. I'll melt.*

The witch sat in the tree until the storm passed. As morning neared, she found she could fly, but just a little bit. Her control was damaged beyond repair by the lightning. She could fly in one short burst, and then the flying was gone. It was all through.

She had to paddle air like crazy. She tumbled back to the tree and wrapped both arms around a branch. She was upside down to the world when she did. Being stuck in a tree was one thing. It was embarrassing. But being a witch stuck upside down was downright degrading. It took some fancy legwork to get herself pointed the right way again. Wet leaves stuck to her hair. A twig had scratched her face. Her cheek bled.

The witch cursed the tree. She shouldn't have done that. Witch-cursed trees sometimes live forever. And even if they die, they don't fall down.

An hour before dawn, she tried to fly again. She managed a little better this time but discovered she hit an invisible wall of electricity at the outer edge of the spread of roots under the tree. This was what had stopped her before when she tried to fly away from the tree in a straight line. The tree, not the ground, was holding the lightning, she realized. The tree had trapped her.

She cursed the tree again, then told herself she had to stop doing that.

≈ ≈ ≈ ≈

Charley climbed down from the attic and got clean underwear and a pair of jeans from his drawer for Ralph. They were a little too big, but Ralph didn't mind.

In the morning, he folded his old clothes into his blanket, to be carried home later. The day was mostly dry by then. The rain had stopped. They had to go outside right then and look at the tree.

It was a big, old tree. It had seemed closer to the house from the attic window at night. They had to leave Charley's yard and walk through tall, wet weeds to get to it.

The witch saw them coming. That was all she needed, some teenage boys throwing rocks at her. Or worse. She held her breath, closed her eyes, and changed as quickly as she could into a cat. It wasn't as easy as it looked. Sometimes, she got headaches when she changed back to a woman. High in the tree was a hollow where two branches formed. It was just big enough to hold a cat, if she was careful with her tail.

"I saw her here as we were coming, but now she's gone," Charley said. "You saw her, too, didn't you?"

"No," Ralph said. To keep from getting hit, he quickly added, "I wasn't looking."

"She was up there, all right. In a white dress, with that long black hair."

"There's nothing here, Charley."

"You saw her. You saw her just like I did. You saw her last night, and she was here in the tree this morning."

"Last night was just a dream. I didn't see anything you saw."

Charley wanted to hit him.

Charley and Ralph kicked at a singed branch on the ground. It was burnt black from lightning at the fat end. If they both pulled from the same end, they could drag the branch back to the house.

"Better leave it here," Ralph said.

Charley agreed. Neither boy knew that a piece of lightning wood is lucky. It is said in the South that a toothpick cut from a lightning-struck branch will cure a sore mouth. But the boys had never heard that. A small boat carved from lightning wood never sinks. You can put it on the river, and it will float all the way to the ocean. A dagger made from lightning wood is a powerful weapon. It will kill a vampire or a witch.

The cat watched them leave. It didn't mind being in the tree as much as the witch did. It waited until they went in the house, then changed back. The witch's mind worked better as a woman than as a cat. The headache was worse this time than others. *It will help*, she thought, *if I have something to eat.*

She had an important decision to make. Food was part of it. Her survival was at stake. A witch sitting in a tree would soon be discovered by someone. When people found her there, they would kill her. They would burn the tree down if they had to. There was nothing for a witch to eat in a tree. And she wouldn't be able to cook a thing.

Climbing down was out of the question. The lightning would kill her.

She considered the cat. The only thing she could come up with was to make the change permanent. You aren't given extra lives unless you're a cat for good. She could live in the tree as a cat for quite some time, eat small birds when she could, chipmunks and a squirrel now and then. And bugs. A cat didn't need to eat anything that was cooked to stay alive. A tree in Louisiana could provide a perpetual feast for a cat. It was a smorgasbord of creepy, crawly living things that cats liked to eat.

The witch cast her spell. It was a very difficult process to become a permanent cat instead of a changeover one. With nine lives, the witch figured she could outlive the tree. It was an old tree to begin with. She hummed and chanted for hours, getting the spell right. The witch meditated her body into near oblivion and became a tiny white speck in a dark world. Then the white dot grew itself into a cat.

Although now forever a cat stuck in a tree, a witch lives inside the thriving animal—a witch that wants out of the tree. Sometimes late at night, every few weeks or every dark moon, a white cat climbs down from the tree just to check. But things are pretty much the same. There's always a flash of lightning and a jarring jolt of electricity that sends the cat quickly back to its hollow to lick its paws, especially the hot one.

Travelers on Highway 190 between Baton Rouge and Livonia sometimes see lightning briefly illuminate a distant tree. The site is not far from were the Hammond house used to be, and not all that far from where Native Americans stuck a red cypress pole decorated with severed animals heads into the ground on the bluff above the Mississippi River.

Camp Cats

≈ ≈ ≈ ≈ ≈ ≈ ≈ ≈ ≈ ≈ ≈ ≈ ≈ ≈ ≈

Some cats go to summer camp. Some are already there.

Pets from home were not allowed at the girls' summer camp in the Blue Ridge Mountains of western North Carolina. Most of the younger campers brought favored stuffed animals to decorate their cabin bunk beds on Black Mountain.

When Katie was ten, she brought a ceramic cat to camp. The tall porcelain animal seemed out of place with the plush teddy bears and stuffed bunnies that rested on the other girls' bunk-bed pillows in her cabin.

Although of small stature, Katie had a huge smile for everyone. She had brown hair and green-gold eyes. She cried sometimes when she talked about her real cat, Samantha. A sleek white cat with four large tan spots, Samantha was a

80   Camp Cats

traditional domestic harlequin cat that had been Katie's companion throughout her childhood.

Katie loved her cabin mates and loved camp. She almost never cried at camp, except when she talked about Samantha.

Her parents had placed Samantha's ashes inside the porcelain cat and sealed the bottom with green felt. The first year she brought her cat's ashes to camp, Katie wanted to show Samantha where she'd been in the summers when she wasn't at home. She carried the porcelain cat to the camp teepee, the totem pole, the archery range, the lake. And she brought it to the stables so the ceramic cat, with Samantha inside, could say hello to her favorite white horse, Henry Lee. She also set it in her lap at every campfire so her cat could hear the stories and listen to the camp songs.

Katie brought the ceramic cat to camp every year after that. At one campfire each camp session, she stood and showed her porcelain cat to the other girls. She told them who was inside, and that Samantha, her deceased harlequin cat, loved being at girls' camp at much as she herself did.

She explained to them that she couldn't take Samantha to school because the mean kids would laugh at her. There were no mean kids around a campfire at camp, she told them. That's why she and Samantha loved being there.

Other girls agreed. In turn, they stood and told their own stories of pets they loved that had died. They spoke softly of loss. Sometimes, a tearful camper would find the courage to speak of a deceased parent or sibling.

Everyone felt closer after Katie talked about her porcelain cat at campfire. The Black Mountain camp for girls awarded white feathers to campers who showed leadership skills and were well liked by the other campers. Every year at camp, Katie and her porcelain cat won a white feather. The blossoming young lady wore the feather proudly around her neck in honor of her childhood cat.

Her last year at camp, when Katie was sixteen, they changed the name of her cabin to Samantha Cat.

Katie remained friends throughout her life with women she had met at girls' camp. She and a few others pooled their resources and sponsored the cost for a girl from an economically challenged family to attend camp free each summer.

Katie died in her early thirties in a car wreck. She had loved nothing more than camp. Her memories of camp were her favorite of all.

Soon after Katie's untimely death, her parents visited the mountain camp at the end of summer. Katie's ashes were placed in the final council fire, along with the ashes from Katie's porcelain cat. It was the most emotional final campfire in the sixty-year history of the girls' camp.

Since that time, a friendly white cat with brown spots has been showing up at the camp. The cat is usually seen in the daytime sitting in the stables or walking by the tennis courts. At night, it has been witnessed sitting in the shadows of trees behind the campfire.

The cat is as real as can be. It is such a gentle, loving cat that it makes friends easily with the young girls. One of the girls will pet it until it purrs happily. Then the cat will scamper off to see what other groups of girls are up to. A few of the older girls know the story of Katie and her porcelain cat. They think the cat is Samantha.

One or two are braver than that. They believe the white

cat with brown spots is Katie coming back to girls' camp.

Someone usually lets it in at night, and the cat almost always ends up on a camper's bunk bed, where it is cuddled and spoiled with attention. The cat has large green-gold eyes. The girl petting the cat notices its brilliant eyes. And in the cat's eyes, at night, is always a reflection of a young girl standing behind the camper. When the girl turns around, no one is there.

No one she can see is there, that is. One or two of the older campers know the truth. This time, it is Katie's cat returning the favor by bringing her young mistress to camp.

≈ ≈ ≈ ≈

Some cats aren't brought to sleep-away camp by fellow campers. The cats in Otter Creek Park were already there.

Several troublesome cat ghosts are known to haunt a girls' camp there. They all came from the same location, a small homestead cabin somewhere in the twenty-six-hundred-acre wilderness just outside Louisville, Kentucky. The cabin no longer stands.

An old man lived alone in the cabin with a family of cats. Leaving the cabin in a blizzard to cut more wood for the fireplace, the old man grew lost in the blinding snow. He wandered in the wrong direction. Dazed and confused, he collapsed from the cold and died. His body wasn't found until spring.

And neither were the bodies of his cats. The man had latched the door against the winter weather. The fire went out, and the cabin grew quickly cold. The cats called for the old man. No one came. Eventually, the family of cats ended up in the fireplace, but the warmth was gone. The ashes were cold.

The flue was open only slightly to allow the last of the firewood in the cabin to burn slowly. The cats had no way out. They froze to death, falling into their final drowsy sleep curled together in the fireplace.

Eventually, the cabin fell into ruin from neglect. The roof caved in. The stone fireplace and chimney collapsed. The floors rotted away.

Years later, stones from the tumbled-down fireplace were used in the circle of rocks around a campfire at the girls' camp nearby. That's when the trouble began.

Cats that have died from the cold can never quite get warm again. That was certainly true of the old man's blizzard-bound cats.

Year after year, as flames leapt from the campfire in Otter Creek Park, the rocks surrounding the fire warmed up quickly. Young campers have said they saw small clouds of mist rising from some of the rocks. Others have heard faint meows as the rocks grew hot from the fire.

The cat ghosts from the frozen cabin live in the rocks from the tumbled-down fireplace. They are always cold once they spring from the rocks. Year after year, summer after summer, the chilly cats scatter, searching for something to keep them warm.

The cats are seen throughout the duration of the camp, always at a distance, from along the woodland trails. They move silently among the trees and rocks of Otter Creek Park. It looks to startled campers who cross their path as if the cats are wearing the wrong fur. Sometimes, the cats seem to be wearing wigs. Other times, it looks like the animals are wearing fuzzy capes of matted fur that are never the same color as the cats.

Late at night, girls in their camp cabins wake up with a start.

"Ouch!" the girl with the longest hair says first. "Someone pulled my hair!"

Throughout the night, the cats move from cabin to cabin collecting as much human hair as possible, as much as they can get away with, to keep them warm. Other people camping in Otter Creek Park in the summer have similar experiences. But the lost ghost cats prefer the girls' camp. It's a simple matter of supply and demand. After a day of endless activity and excitement, nobody sleeps more soundly than young girls at summer camp.

When the last fire of camp is extinguished and the rocks cool, the cats return to their tumbled-down stones and wait for summer so they can get warm again.

Eat-Your-Face Cat

≈ ≈ ≈ ≈ ≈ ≈ ≈ ≈ ≈ ≈ ≈ ≈ ≈

It has long been a tradition in the South to name your children after somebody or something. Beale Roberts was named after a street in Memphis. His grandmother Magnolia was named after a tree. People who met Beale for the first time thought his name was Bill. Many still do.

Magnolia grew up in Sugar Ditch, so she didn't take much stock in names. There was nothing sweet about Sugar Ditch. Magnolia's daddy and her third husband died on the same day.

They died in a motel fire in Arkansas. The men had been working strawberries over there. A Memphis lawyer went to court over the fire and earned a bunch of money for Magnolia. She moved her two boys and one daughter to a brick house outside town. She kept her husband's car.

But that was some time ago. Magnolia had her children late in life. Beale's mother was just a little girl. The boys were older. The boys moved to Memphis, one at a time, to good jobs in the hospitals there. When you were raised in a good house, you learned to want better things in life than Tunica, Mississippi. Beale's mother stayed behind until she grew up. Then she went to Memphis. She worked as a waitress on Beale Street till five in the morning, got herself pregnant, and came right back to Tunica to find someone to marry her. That was Beale's daddy. He thought Beale's name was Bill, too.

Having her children late in life was a mistake on Magnolia's part. She might as well have been their grandmother. Magnolia ended up living alone. The money was gone, but she still had her house and the old car. She kept the car up because she needed it for church and the stores.

When her health failed, she adopted a cat advertised on the church bulletin board as needing a home. The cat was her family then. She named the cat Robber because he stole food from Magnolia's plate the first day she brought him home. She fed Robber more than she should have because she didn't like eating alone.

Robber didn't mind eating alone, but he died anyway. Right after Magnolia did.

That Monday morning, she put Robber in the car for a trip to the grocery store in town. Her heart felt fluttery. When she climbed into the car and closed the door, Magnolia went dizzy from her head down to her feet. Her heart stopped. It was done.

Robber chewed on her purse the first day. He walked all over that car looking for a way out. There was none.

The second Sunday Magnolia missed church, the preacher came by. He found Magnolia and Robber in the car by following the bad smell in the yard. The cat had chewed off most of Magnolia's face before he died of thirst.

The funeral was a closed-casket one. After Magnolia was in the ground, one of her sons drove the car to his house in Memphis. Everyone agreed that Beale would inherit his grandmother's car when he was old enough.

When Beale was fourteen, he fell in love with girls and cars at the same time. In bed at night, he practiced shifting with his right hand in the standard three-gear H configuration. He'd have to know how in order to get a license. If he got it wrong, the examiner would laugh at him. He moved his left foot from the imaginary clutch, then back again. Beale lifted his right foot off the gas while shifting. He made motor sounds. He switched to a four-gear configuration with Reverse down to the side. His bedcovers were a mess by the time he finished driving.

Beale's mother brought him to her brother's house in Memphis to see the car. His uncle took him for a ride across the Mississippi River and back. The 1956 two-door Chevy Bel Air sparkled like new. There wasn't a scratch on it. Not a single speck of rust. Its V-8 engine had plenty of power.

"Always sat in your grandma's garage," his uncle said. "Runs like new. When you get your license and a job, you can drive it home."

"A job? I've had plenty of jobs."

"A real job, Beale. Have you tried applying to the casinos yet? They hire in the kitchens at sixteen, don't they?"

"I guess so."

"Well, you get a job to help out your momma at home, and we'll see if your grandma's car will start up for you. It won't start for just anyone."

Beale was eighteen and working full time at one of the casinos in North Tunica when his uncle finally said he could have the Bel Air. Beale couldn't wait to be rid of the second-hand Dodge Shadow he drove to work and back.

He sat in his grandmother's car in his uncle's driveway in Memphis and admired his hands on the red steering wheel. The insides of the doors were red tuck-and-roll upholstery. He rolled down the driver's window and stuck his elbow outside.

"Start her up," the uncle said.

The 1956 Chevy purred. His uncle grinned. He'd be glad to get rid of it. The car gave him the creeps.

"Before you drive home, there are some things you need to know, Beale," he said.

"Yes, sir?"

The chrome hood ornament looked like an airplane. It sparkled in the sunlight. Beale couldn't wait to take off.

"Well, I guess you know how your grandma died. She died sitting in this car. That cat ate her face. Ate her face clean off. You know about all that, don't you?"

"I do."

"I don't know how, but that cat is still in the car. You'll hear him making noise when you're riding around. Backseat, front seat. I don't know how. He's just there."

Beale thought his uncle was nuts.

"I worked two shifts one weekend at the hospital, and when we had a break I lay down in the car in the parking lot. I was going to sleep through my lunch hour. I started to doze off, and that cat bit my ear pretty good, Beale. I thought a bee had me, so I swatted at it. My ear was bleeding, but it didn't hurt too bad. I tried to go back to sleep, and each time I dozed off that cat ghost took a bite of my face."

Beale nodded slowly, trying not to laugh.

"I have to tell you this. I know it doesn't sound quite right, but I have to tell you. Don't be sleeping in the car, that's all. That cat will eat your face off if you do. He's a hungry little ghost, Beale, with razor claws and sharp teeth. If you fall asleep, that cat will think you're dead and will eat your face off. I'd have given you the car sooner, but I didn't know how to say it to you."

"Won't be any sleeping done in this car," Beale promised.

On the drive south to Tunica, Beale supposed everyone in the small towns along the Mississippi believed in ghosts. Every bayou had one or two walking around in it at night, if you listened to the old folks. They were all crazy about ghosts. There was supposed to be a woman out by Anderson Bayou who walked across the road at night, carrying her head under one arm. When you drove by her, the head would end up in your backseat and start talking to you. But that was only when the moon was full. Beale guessed his uncle was no different from the others, to believe in such things.

Beale loved his grandma's Bel Air. When he parked the classic two-door at the casino, people of all types would come over to talk to him about it. When he got off work, Beale found notes tucked under the windshield wiper from people who wanted to buy the Bel Air. They wrote down their phone numbers.

Nights off, Beale ate at Church's Chicken but parked at the Sonic Drive-In to show off the car. He sat with his elbow out the driver's window. Sometimes, he ordered a Coke. The local girls circling through would honk. A car filled with high-school girls would pull up alongside him in the next slot.

"Do you have a girlfriend?" they'd ask.

Then one of them would get into Beale's car to go for a ride.

Beale liked driving them on Beat Line because it had good lights and everyone could see he was with somebody. He'd put his right arm across the back of the front seat and drive with his left elbow out the window, keeping his fingers on the steering wheel. He'd cross over to the old Main Street and drive real slow up past Magnolia, then circle the block at Edwards Street and do it over again. His favorite trick was to drive with his lights off in Kestevan Alley. He'd ease on up to Café Marie's, where he'd pop the lights on and turn back to Main. The girls thought that was dangerous.

Everyone in town parked at the Sonic at night when it closed. They stayed there to talk. The girls would walk from car to car, showing off their hairdos and their clothes. They stayed there until the police drove through, then everyone divided up into cars and went back to Main.

One night, the girl at Beale's passenger door was almost too drunk to stand up. Her name was Amber, and she'd ridden with Beale before.

Amber said she wanted to go for a ride. He didn't mind. When she was drinking, Amber liked to neck, and that was just fine with Beale. She told him she liked his car because it had big seats.

When girls like Amber were in the car, Beale had a place to drive way out behind the bayou off Fox Island Road.

"Beale, do you ever think of marrying anyone?"

"No," he said. He'd seen women at the casino he would like to have married, though. Most of them already were.

Amber shrugged. "I guess no one thinks that way anymore."

Her boyfriend in Memphis didn't want to get married. Neither did her boyfriend in Arkansas. Neither one came to Tunica as often as they used to. Amber leaned her head against the window and felt the motor vibrate the car as they drove through the darkness until Beale found a place to park.

He left the car running while they were parked on the old briar road behind the bayou. It was where people came to pick wild blackberries in summer. The air smelled like fish. The exhaust pipes hummed. Beale raced the motor once or twice in Park, then let it idle. It drowned out the noise from frogs and bugs.

By the time Beale climbed back into the driver's seat, it was after midnight. Amber stayed in the backseat, straightening her clothes.

As soon as he was on Fox Island Road again, Beale felt Amber kick the back of his seat.

"Stop that," he said, "or I'll end up driving us off the road."

When he looked over his shoulder into the backseat, Beale saw Amber curled up asleep. She slept on her side with her knees drawn up, dead to the world. She must have passed out, he guessed. She'd been as drunk as he'd ever seen a girl. Beale glanced back once or twice more, hoping she'd be able to walk when it came time to drop her off. He didn't plan on keeping her all night.

He finally got a better look as he neared the edge of town. That was when he saw Amber's face. Long, bloody cuts had been scratched into her face from eyebrow to chin. Her mouth was hanging open. Her tongue was gone.

Beale pulled over to the side of the road as quickly as he could. When he opened the driver's door, the dome light came on. Then the worst of it happened. Amber sat up in the seat in a sudden rush. She wanted to wake up, but it was too late. Her mouth was filled with blood. She tossed her head from side to side, and pieces of her face came away.

As pieces of her face were bitten off, they disappeared. Her nose came off. A bloody hole was above her lips.

Beale yelled for it to stop. He pushed himself quickly out of the car. He nearly fell over backwards on his bottom but held the door to right himself. Beale wanted to pull the driver's seat forward to get back there, but he froze in place. His hand wouldn't move to help her. He couldn't make it move.

Her lips came off in little bites that spread quickly across the rest of her face. It happened as fast as a car going ninety down the highway. It was as if a hundred cats were eating Amber's face. Her eyeballs came out of her head. They made little popping sounds. Bitten in half, they were quickly gone. Her ears, the same.

It stopped for a minute when her face was gone. Beale pulled the driver's seat forward and stared into the back, mortified. Her face was a bloody pulp with no skin at all. He could see the bone edges where her upper teeth fit, and the bare bone at her jaw. Amber looked like she was smiling without a face.

Beale shook her by the arms. He heard a cat meow. But when he looked for the cat, nothing was there. He stared hard at Amber again. Either she was dead or he was dreaming. For only a moment, he didn't know which.

The car was still running. Amber was dead.

Then the eating started again. Amber's fingers came off her hands. He could see it happening. The flesh of her fingers disappeared until her hands were only bones. Her neck ripped open, and the flesh curled away. Beale let go of her and backed away from the car. He sat down hard on his rear end, his eyes staring wide open at the 1956 Bel Air.

It happened so fast that he couldn't believe it was real. When it seemed like it must be through, he got back in the car. What was left of Amber was spread across the backseat.

He drove long, slow circles around town. He drove to the airport and back. Beale thought he might be in shock, and that was why he couldn't do anything. All the while, he listened to the snapping and gnawing of bones. The cat ghost was hungrier now than in real life. It had eaten all of Amber.

He finally drove around behind the Sonic Drive-In and put his grandmother's car in Park. He opened the car door. The dome light came on. Heavy with fear and dread, Beale climbed out of the car and leaned back in to see what might be done. He had to take her somewhere. He had to do something.

Amber was entirely gone. Nothing was left but her clothes and shoes. Not a speck of blood or skin or bone anywhere. Her skull and teeth were gone. The cat had eaten everything human.

Beale put her clothes and shoes in the trunk and closed the

lid. He walked to the big green dumpster to take a leak. No sooner was he finished and zipped up than a spotlight came on, blinding him.

Beale put his arm over his face so he could see.

"Come over here," a male voice said.

The spotlight went off. Beale walked to the police car.

"Do you know a girl named Amber Monroe? She's about your age."

"Yes, sir, I think I do. But I haven't seen her lately. Is something wrong?"

"Probably called her boyfriend in Memphis to come down to get her. Her parents said she didn't come home tonight. They call us all the time."

Beale nodded.

"It's against the law to pee back here, you know?"

"No, sir, I didn't know that. I apologize."

"That's all right then. Just don't be doing it often, Beale. You better get on home now. Don't want you worrying your momma over little things."

Beale drove out of town on Fox Island Road instead. It was quiet out that way. He kept his elbow out the window. If he told anybody, they wouldn't believe him. He'd get in trouble of some kind for having her clothes, but without a body it wouldn't be murder. They'd hound him to say each place he and Amber had been. And they wouldn't find her anyway. No one ever would.

He got to work early the next day and used the phone on his break to call some of the numbers that had been placed under the wiper of his car. The first one he called was the man who ended up buying the Bel Air from Beale.

"That's my grandmother's name on the title. It was always her car."

"Anything else I should know?"

"It has a cat ghost that lives in the seats. Won't bother anyone unless you go to sleep in the car. He was my grandma's cat. He died when she did."

The man stared at him.

"Don't let anyone go to sleep in the car." Beale had to tell him. "The cat will eat their face if you do."

The man laughed.

"They all have a story to tell," he said, shaking Beale's hand. "These old cars all have a story or two."

Cat Shine

≈ ≈ ≈ ≈ ≈ ≈ ≈ ≈ ≈ ≈ ≈ ≈

They had to tear down the outhouses and build new ones at the Free Will Baptist church out in the Edgefield district. The good Southern Baptists there were getting the ghost in the wrong way at those outhouses back behind the church. The preacher blamed it all on Gedde Hahn. But the preacher had a little bit to do with it himself.

Gedde Hahn hated his wife. He hated his neighbors. And he hated the man in the moon.

He hadn't set out to hate people so. They just seemed to deserve it. When he came home from the War Between the States, having served in Hampton's Legion through to the end, he hated that both his brothers were dead. They'd been killed in battle and by army fevers, along with almost everyone else in South Carolina except the generals, who were all lawyers to begin with. Lawyers could live through about anything, if someone else would die in their place.

When Confederate general Martin Witherspoon Gary returned to Edgefield, Gedde found out he hated him for certain. Gary was just another lawyer trying to tell people how they should vote. According to the general, they should vote for him.

Gedde had a cat named Lee, and that was about the only being he liked to spend time with those days. Lee was gray all over, and Gedde thought he should be named something else, but everyone thought the world of Robert E. Lee. Gedde had never met the man. But if he had been introduced to Robert E. Lee, Gedde was sure he would have hated him. But since he didn't hate him yet, Gedde named his gray cat Lee.

The family land was all his now, 160 acres above West Stores Crossing. It was mostly scrub trees and brush, far too much of it covered with woods. His wife made a garden and kept the house. Gedde didn't know how she managed it, and he didn't care. He didn't like her much, and as best he could tell she didn't like him.

He was still a young man and needed a better way than crops to make a living. He put a few acres in corn but rarely messed with them. He grew his beard.

Gedde had learned to make pots and jugs when he was young, while his older brothers took care of the farm. He still knew how. Gedde had two good hands for it. He made a clay smoking pipe and kept it in his mouth almost all the time, to keep from telling people, and his wife, how much he hated them.

The slaves left the potteries at the end of the war. All of them up and walked away. General Gary didn't want them around if they could vote. He would have told them to leave, but they were already gone. Gedde saw his opportunity was to make pots cheaper than the factory potters could. They were lazy no-accounts over at Pottersville, and he hated every last one of them. They once had the slaves throwing those big jars together for them, and turning the jugs in the fire when it was at its hottest. They were all too lazy to do it for themselves now.

Lee stood guard atop the toolhouse while Gedde built a large pottery shed. Then he and Lee rode his wagon to the old Modoc camps near the Savannah River and loaded it with clay. He could dig clay almost anywhere, but the Modoc people had already processed the dirt and chips out of theirs, so he could start working right away. He hated them, though, for charging him so much. Neither he nor Lee said a word on the haul home. The next batch, he would use his own clay.

He dug a groundhog kiln the size of four graves. Lee watched him every step of the way. Gedde bought bricks for the lining and the roof of it. He filled washtubs with water and worked the clay on a treadle wheel. He practiced cutting lids of clay to match the storage jars he made. Half-gallon on up, jars for pickling, for salting meat, for storing lard. Jars for about anything.

When Gedde was done with those, he made jugs. The handles were trickier, but he picked up the skill on his own. The jugs didn't have to be as big. The jugs were for holding vinegar, wine, molasses, and spirituous liquors. Lots of boys were making spirituous liquors after the war. He tried pitchers and didn't like it much. He did up a handful of pans, and some bowls for kitchen mixing. Gedde made a few tobacco pipes. He wanted one for himself that was glazed on the outside and wouldn't get so hot when he smoked it.

The glaze was a messy job, but an important one. Gedde ground up feldspar with a stone and added wood ashes, lime, and any sand he could find. He wasn't sure what color the syrupy glaze would turn out until he fired it, but at the beginning it was green. The firing took three days. It was awful work, and Gedde had to go at it flat out to keep enough wood for the flames.

He hated the pieces that broke in the fire and cussed them good. But most of them didn't break. Gedde made them thick to keep that from happening. The glaze was different on some, tan and brown, olive and brown, gray and brown. Most of the top runs were brown and looked like tobacco juice. The glaze cooked hard as stone. He had to use a grinding wheel on the bottoms where it ran down and made lips around the edges.

Gedde Hahn went to church to let as many people know as he could that his pots and jugs were done. He loaded one of each on the wagon. His wife came along. They might not let him in without her. Lee guarded the works at home.

"Nobody's going to steal anything," his wife said. "They're all in church."

"The people who don't steal are in church," Gedde corrected her. Then again, she might be right. Gedde hated the idea of that.

Gedde had listened to plenty of Episcopal sermons in the camps during the War Between the States. The Virginia preachers spoke softly of duty and sacrifice and made complicated definitions out of parts of the Bible that Gedde had never read. Some things paralleled some other things, he learned, and parallels amounted to tantamount. The fact he couldn't disagree with a one of the preachers made him like them less. He had quit listening altogether after Second Manassas.

The Free Will Baptist preacher, Brother Blaine, was different from the Episcopalians. He said his sermons simple and plain. And about the only Bible Brother Blaine knew was the Ten Commandments, although he added several by the time he was through. You could hate him right off the mark, if you wanted to.

"Lord," he said, "it is a sin to want things!"

It was a sin to drink. It was a sin to smoke. And, he shouted, it was a sin to eat.

It was a sin to eat when other people were hungry. Gedde didn't hate him for saying that. *I eat when I'm hungry*, he thought, *not when other people are.*

Money was a sin, too. And to prove it, the deacons passed the bowls to help you get rid of yours. The next time he came with a wagon of pots and jugs, he'd have to get to church sooner, before the money ran out when Brother Blaine took it all.

When it came to the Bible, Gedde concluded that the only thing left for a man to decide was which sins he'd take on and which ones he would leave for others. It was handy, having a list shouted out for you, so you could choose.

Gedde's pots and jugs were good ones, heavy and stout, and word spread around West Stores Crossing and beyond. Over time, he sold most of them. He made money. And then he made more pots. It was hard work, but he was used to that. He made more money when he dug into a hillside on his place and began processing his own clay. People in the district ended up with plenty of storage jars and lard pots.

Before two years were out, Gedde learned that the demand was in jugs.

The boys who cooked up illegal liquor ordered them in advance. They paid more for jugs than anyone paid for pots and jars. They paid even more when Lee made the half-gallon jugs with the bottoms twice as thick and curved up from the middle a small ways in. They said it was to keep the bottoms extra strong because the jugs got dropped and plunked down hard on rocks and benches and stumps and things. Gedde knew better. They wanted those particular half-gallon jugs because they held pretty much less than a half-gallon.

Gedde Hahn marked his jugs for the liquor trade by cutting into the surface of the clay with an awl before the glazing and firing. He knew which ones were which from then on. He came up with the idea to write things in the clay with his awl. Gedde got a kick out of that. His favorite was when he wrote "Ain't No Sin" on some he took to his church the first Sunday after a firing.

Lee got old watching Gedde make jugs. He'd move his gray tail in time while the wheel spun. But otherwise, Lee looked bored by it all.

"Let's do something new, Lee," Gedde said around the glazed clay pipe in his mouth. "The boys that put up shine are paying me twice what anyone else can pay for a jug." He stared hard at the cat. The cat stared back. "That means they are making more money than anyone. That means they are making more money that I am. I hate that."

He put all his tools on his wagon and hauled it up to

the back of his land, where he cut clay from the hillsides. He already had dug a big clay cave in one of those hidden hills. Gedde built his still in there. A man couldn't see a thing from anywhere, for all the trees. He well knew he could make more jugs than one still could use up. So he put another still right next to the first. And then he built a third. Much as he hated to, Gedde planted more corn.

Gedde became the first man in all of the Edgefield district to make his own squeezins and his own jugs to put them in. He kept his liquor pure. He put in sugar, of course, and a smidgen of molasses to add color and a hint of taste besides copper pan. Gedde had learned to mix for color by making glaze.

He sold his spirituous liquor for less than the old boys could. Gedde had made his way in the world. A liquor cooker couldn't buy an empty jug from Gedde Hahn anymore.

Gedde went to church more often. He put a canvas cover on the wares in the wagon. He wrote some of the words that he heard at church on his jugs. "The Lord Taketh" was one he used. Then he wrote on the other side, "Drink Fast."

Lee enjoyed watching the stills cook. The small fires flickered and licked at the air. They didn't drive him off like the kiln fires did. The copper tubs pinged when they got hot and cooled off, which kept his attention. The clay was cool for a cat to stretch out on.

Lamp and ladle ledges were carved all along the sides of that clay cave. One day, Gedde moved a ladle from one clay ledge to another while stirring hot mash. Maybe Lee was too old to take note of it. When Gedde was out at the wagon getting sugar, the gray cat leapt to a ledge from another one and ran into that ladle. He came off the clay and fell into the cooking mash. Lee died right away. He sunk down in and stayed.

Gedde hated that the most. It broke his heart to lose his friend that way.

A cat distilled was to Gedde's mind a cat taken care of, same as if he'd been cremated or buried. He had an idea for a grave marker, and he put his hands to it.

He wet the clay and threw the jugs on the wheel lickety-split. He worked a good thick lip on each one. He marked a set of cat whiskers with the awl into each of them. Gedde ran the glaze from top to bottom. He fired the kiln.

Four day later, those jugs had cooled.

When the half-gallon whiskers jugs were filled and cork-ed, Gedde raked out the mash and let it dry. He layered it in a canvas tote and carried it by Jakob Jaynes's farm as slop for the hog.

It was a cold autumn come down. Gedde rode the wagon to West Stores Crossing in the middle of the week. People called it "airish" when it got this cool. Gedde wore a slouch hat to hold his hair on. The crops were out, and the gardens were done. The harvests were in. It was cold enough to drink, and everybody wanted some. Gedde parked his wagon in the road. His beard tilted in the wind. It came straight down from the north, where it was airish most every night.

A man could have a sample if he asked for it. Gedde kept a little liquor in an open pottery jar. They'd hoot and holler and stamp the ground. Gedde kept his pipe in his mouth and thought Lee would be proud.

"Don't break that jug. You can use it again."

That was the only thing he said to them.

He sold every jug of cat shine he had on his wagon.

When Gedde got out of bed Sunday morning to stoke the fireplace and put a pot of coffee in at the edge, he heard a cat meow. It sounded like Lee. Every time he took a step, he heard the meow. His wife snored away in the covers. He hated the way she snored and didn't like sticking around. Still, he looked for Lee where he heard the meow loudest. He looked under the bed.

A silliness came over him for doing that. Nothing was under the bed but the chamber pot on the low side, where his wife slept. He hated her for weighing the bed down like that.

Gedde combed his beard for church and put a brand-new pipe in his mouth. He wrapped up and tramped out to the pottery shed. He had kept one jug for himself. The rest were sold. Lee's passing was being marked by many men in the district, more than would ever attend a funeral for a cat, he bet.

He swirled that jug in his hand. It was lighter than it should have been. It sloshed when it should have been full. His wife must have had the cork out of this one. Gedde wondered how long she'd been doing that. It made him smile to understand why she had taken to singing late at night sometimes before coming to bed. He liked her for it. And he wouldn't hate church as much from now on, knowing that the properly dressed woman with her hair tied up sitting next to him was a sinner, same as he was.

Uncorking the bottle, Gedde heard that long meow. The whiskey he had made was part Lee. There wasn't a cat in the world that liked being bottled up. He took a good long swig. He put the cork back in.

Gedde waited, but not long at all, and pulled the cork out.

Meow!

This was fun. Gedde grinned and danced a bit. He hadn't danced since before the war. He put the cork in four or five more times. Every time he got it out, Lee let loose with a healthy meow. Gedde laughed so hard his pipe dropped out of his mouth.

In a little, he came out into the wind, wobbling some. Gedde stumbled around to the back of the shed and leaned one arm against the planking to relieve himself. As he did, Lee meowed, long and loud. The dead cat wouldn't stop meowing when he hit the open air. That explained the chamber pot. Gedde laughed so hard he fell down. He rolled on the ground in his overalls, laughing at Lee. For a good ten minutes, he didn't hate anything or anyone. The war was over for Gedde and for everyone who had died scared and sick and away from home. The war was over for every wretched one who died in pain.

Little pieces of leaves were in his beard when he carried the jug back into the house that morning for pancakes and coffee.

Gedde Hahn couldn't stop grinning long enough to go to church that Sunday. He danced his wife around the house instead.

≈ ≈ ≈ ≈

Two weeks later, a man in a suit and tie stepped down from the train in Trenton, South Carolina. He asked to hire a carriage to take him to the Jakob Jaynes farm. He wore a waxed mustache and a derby hat. He said he was with the Southern Circus. He carried a cane with a jade elephant on top.

The ticket clerk told him the farm was on the other side of Edgefield, and that he had just heard about it himself.

"How long will it take to have me there, if you don't mind my asking?"

"You're too late, if you come to buy those pigs," the clerk said. "They stopped meowing more than a day ago."

"I see," the man in the suit said. He pushed the front edge of his derby up with the head of his cane. He leaned forward and spoke softly. "Do you think any of that whiskey is left?"

"Don't matter." The clerk smiled. "Gedde Hahn made those jugs to be reused. Any whiskey you put in them comes out the same."

The new outhouses at the Free Will Baptist church in the Edgefield district had a sign on each door painted by Brother Blaine. "No Hard Lickuor of Any Kind," the signs said. That was the Eleventh Commandment in those parts.

Bump-Heads Cat

Most people know that witches can see at night, but they don't know why. Witches can see at night because they trade eyes with cats. It's easier than flying with flashlights or lanterns through the darkness.

Jeanie Epps read about witches in England and Japan. Witches in England boil eggs to cast spells. Their eyes look like eggshells. The witches in Japan are all women who are ghosts. They wear their hair undone and have no feet. They glide with their arms held out. They have no eyes, only teeth.

The world around, you know you're in a witch's house when you see a pair of human eyes in a glass of water by the bed. The witch is off somewhere with a pair of cat's eyes in her head. You best get out. No one should steal the witch's eyes,

Jeanie knew, or the witch would need to replace them. And dead eyes wouldn't do.

A witch uses her cat to find new eyes for her.

An area not far from where Jeanie lived was known as Dogtown before it became part of Nashville, Tennessee. Dogtown was full of witches and drunks. A witch who was a prostitute put spells on men to make them think she was beautiful and young. Sometimes, the spell wore off too soon, which wasn't good for customer relations. Once, a disgruntled and drunken gambler came back and stole her eyes while she was asleep. From then on, she needed human eyes to see. The problem was they'd last only a week before drying out, so she was in rather constant want of fresh eyes.

The sightless witch taught her cat to get eyes for her. When the drunks fell down in the street at two or three in the morning, the cat would come out of the shadows from under a wooden porch along a dirt street. The cat walked softly to one fallen drunk after another, putting its nose to each man's face to see if he would wake up easily.

When he didn't, the cat went to work. Using furry paws so soft you could barely feel a thing, the cat milked both eyeballs from inside their sockets. When the cat had them all the way out, dangling on their sinewy cords of pink flesh, it extended its claws and cut them cleanly off, one after another. It escaped through the night at a silent run, a human eyeball dangling from each side of its mouth. The witch could see for a few days and became a beautiful young prostitute again. She learned to be careful not to put the eyes in upside down.

"Bull malarkey!" Rusty said when Jeanie was through telling him about it.

"How do you know it's not true? You've never seen a prostitute. You don't know whose eyes they wear."

Jeanie's cousin didn't know for sure what a prostitute was, except that he wasn't supposed to say the word around adults, which made it interesting. He liked Jeanie, and he liked being at her place. He learned all sorts of things.

Just off Brick Church Road north of Nashville was a little farm valley called Willow Creek. Most pets in Willow Creek were house cats. They stalked through the yards and fields like all cats do when given the opportunity. The family cats would loll around on a porch or under a tree and let you look at them. One big cat in Willow Creek, however, was just a blur.

Jeanie Epps grew up there. Her family had a large red-shingled house, two pastures, and two hay barns, along with a good-sized yard that was as pretty as a park. Jeanie was a tomboy when she was younger, about Rusty's age. She had many fun places for her girlhood adventures. She could wander pretty much where she wanted.

Only one place was off-limits. It was the old widow's farm. She'd died, and the farm was in disrepair. The house had fallen in, and the barn was about to. A fence was along her parcel. Jeanie's parents had forbidden her to ever go on the other side of that fence. They pretty much knew she would explore the old barn at the widow's house. Falling-down barns were dangerous.

"Just don't you do it," her mother said. "And don't tell Rusty to do it when he's here."

"I don't tell him to do anything," Jeanie said.

So she did. Jeanie waited until her cousins were visiting and the adults had gone into town. Rusty didn't know the rule about the fence, so he couldn't be blamed. She could say she had to go after him. If caught, that is. But she wouldn't be caught.

Jeanie stirred sugar and a dead bug into a cup of coffee one of the parents had left behind.

"Here, drink this," she told her cousin. "You'll need it where we're going."

She was careful how they slipped away from the house that day. Jeanie waited until the younger kids were watching cartoon videos. She and Rusty went out the back, and she didn't let the screen door bang. Jeanie raced across the pasture, Rusty right behind her.

"A prostitute is a woman who sleeps with a man for money," she told him. "I couldn't say it in the house with the little kids there."

"I know!" Rusty lied. He wondered how much money he would have to pay to watch a woman sleeping. Why would she have to charge him anything? "Why don't you let me see you sleep some? You could go to sleep right now if you laid down."

Jeanie laughed. "I'm not sleeping for you, Rusty Wheeler. You're too young."

"Am not."

"Besides, girls don't sleep for their cousins. It's wrong."

They stopped at the fence, then went right over it.

"Are we going to smoke?" Rusty wanted to know.

"Maybe. If you aren't a baby, we will."

Jeanie wanted to look around the widow's farm and see what they could find. She wanted something to hide in her room. She didn't know what, though.

"If we don't smoke, what are we going to do?"

"There's something in this old lady's barn I'm not supposed to see."

"What?"

"I won't know until I see it," Jeanie said.

"Is it big?"

"I don't know! Now, shut up and come along."

"I will if you kiss my arm again."

"That was just once to show you how it's done. I'm not doing it again. Rusty, you're dumb. Hurry up, now."

Rusty didn't budge. Jeanie wanted him to come with her, so he decided to hold out.

She walked back and stood in front of him.

"Okay," she said. "Pull your shirt up to your neck, and I'll put a hickey on your chest."

When he did as he was told, she punched him right in the ribs.

Rusty fell backwards. It hurt, and he wanted to cry. But if he did, Jeanie would call him a baby and would never let him watch her sleep. Rusty followed her, but not too quickly. He was disappointed in their outing. It was a lot of work trudging around farm fields.

"Where's the old lady?" he finally asked.

"She's in the graveyard, if you have to know. Now, come on!"

The weeds were thick and tall in the field on the other side of the fence, and it was a hike to the widow's barn. They found an old tractor path, and that made it easier. Jeanie stopped to pull a cocklebur off her shoelace.

"There's a bee on your butt," Rusty said.

Jeanie stopped walking and turned around.

"There is not," she said.

"I know. I'm supposed to slap your bottom after I say it."

"You touch my bottom, Rusty Wheeler, and I'm breaking your arm."

Jeanie managed the hike without further physical assault upon her younger cousin. She'd trained him well.

The old barn was great. It was better than she'd hoped. It leaned far to one side under its roof. It was near to completely falling in. It was a hundred years old at least. The door was entirely off. Shafts of light shot through holes in the roof and where boards were missing.

"It's full of snakes," Rusty said. "I'll wait here."

He tucked his shirt in. Rusty didn't want anything crawling inside his shirt. He pulled his socks up over the legs of his Levi's. It looked pretty stupid, but Rusty knew that snakes lived in barns. He'd been in barns before. Just hanging around the outsides of barns, you risked having a snake find you.

Jeanie walked into the barn.

"Come on," she called. "You aren't a sissy, are you? You're a sissy, Rusty Wheeler, and a big baby, too."

Rusty reluctantly followed her in. He hated it when she called him a baby just because she was older than he was. It smelled bad inside the barn. It smelled like poop, and the air was full of dirt. He could see dirt moving in the light shafts. Moldy, hay-covered wooden steps were to one side, and a broken ladder to the loft. Everything looked awfully old and maybe rotted. An old pair of gloves was on the floor. A hat covered with spider webs hung on a hook. The loft was full of old hay bales.

"They just left everything here when she died," Jeanie said.

She looked around. Then she pointed at a board on the wall. "Grab that hat and put it on."

"No!" Rusty said. He shivered.

"Go on, now. Do it, you big baby!"

He wasn't about to touch the thing. "What are we looking for anyway?"

"An old hunting knife, maybe," Jeanie said. "A gun."

"There's no gun."

"Might be in the loft."

"Maybe we better go. It smells like snakes."

"You going to start crying? Might be old fishing stuff we can use for ourselves. Just start looking."

Rusty picked up a broken hoe handle and poked at the clumps of hay on the floor.

A big cat jumped from the loft above them. Rusty saw it coming and tried to yell. When he turned to start running, his shoe came off. Jeanie jumped to the side, and the cat missed her. It looked too big to her to be a cat. In a blur, it was gone.

They were both outside the barn in a hurry. They ran about twenty steps and stopped. It was sunny out, and nothing was chasing them now.

"My shoe," Rusty moaned. "It's inside."

"What was that, a wolf? So, go get it."

"I'm not going in there. Didn't you see that cat? It didn't have eyes."

"That was a cat? No way. It was too big for a cat. Missed me by a hair."

"It was a cat," Rusty insisted. "And it didn't have eyes, just empty holes in its head. You didn't even see it."

"If it was just a cat, I'm going back in. Barn cats run off like that. They're afraid of you. It was running off, that's all. Are you sure it was a cat?"

"I'm not going in again. I'm going home."

"What about your shoe?"

"I don't care. I'll say I lost it somewhere."

"You going to hop all the way back to the house?"

"If I have to."

"All right then, I'll get it for you. You're a big baby, you know that? It was just a cat, and it had eyes. You heard me say that about witches in Dogtown, and you just thought it didn't have eyes. Barn cats have eyes, Rusty Wheeler. They all do."

Jeanie walked back to the barn. That's when she learned the truth about a witch's cat that wants a pair of eyes. It leapt right on her, full into her chest, and knocked her down. Jeanie screamed when eighteen pounds of matted fur and bone slammed into her. She lost her breath when she hit the ground. It hurt. It hurt worse than getting punched in the chest.

The old blind cat was on her in an instant. The witch's cat bumped heads with Jeanie, just like any cat will do. She still couldn't get her breath. It hardly hurt, though, when Jeanie's eyes popped out of their sockets and into the cat's. The cat's extended claws sliced through the eye cords in a flash. And then the cat was off her as quick as that.

Rusty threw his other shoe when Jeanie screamed. He ran as hard as he knew how to get back to the house. He banged his toe climbing the fence.

≈ ≈ ≈ ≈

After two years of attending a special school for the blind, glass eyes in her face instead of real ones, Jeanie telephoned her cousin. He was older than the last time she called him. He would help.

"I know what to do," Jeanie told him. "You come out here and help me find that cat. If I bump heads back, I'll be able to see again."

"Naw," Rusty said. "I don't think so."

"I'll show you how to kiss with your tongue," she offered.

"No. I'm still a big baby," he said.

He disconnected the call. He'd said the same thing before to her. Every time she called.

Sometimes, through no fault of her own, a witch doesn't make it home when she goes out at night. Some poor cat has to go through the rest of its life without eyeballs unless it can find someone to bump heads with, like the cats around Dogtown do.

Ice-Cold Cat

It was too hot to kiss.

The sun shimmered, rising early on yet another long summer day in Decatur County, Georgia. It was too hot for young lovers to be outdoors and do anything much more than look at each other. Holding hands made your fingers sweat.

David Hyatt had a cool idea. He drove out of Climax, Georgia, with his girlfriend in the passenger seat of his Toyota pickup. He worked nights all summer. The heat of the day was all that remained for his dates with DeeAnna.

"I'd rather go to the movies than have a picnic," she said.

David would rather the two of them were alone that Saturday. The air conditioning filled the cab with noise but made it possible to sit in the truck without your shirt sticking to your back. The dashboard, taking sunlight through the windshield, was too hot to touch.

"It's not a picnic," David said. "It's a camping trip."

David had packed two flashlights for their outing. The sleeping bags were in the back of the trunk. An ice cooler you could pull on wheels was packed with soda pop and bottled beer.

"It's not a camping trip, David, unless you stay overnight."

"Day camp," he mumbled, knowing she couldn't hear him over the air conditioning.

"When we get there, I'm sticking my feet in the ice chest," she said. Because he had said they were going camping, Dee-Anna wore sneakers instead of flip-flops. Her feet were hot. "I don't feel like traipsing around."

David's destination was an opening between two large rocks. It was one of the numerous back entries into the winding labyrinths of the Climax Caverns. More than seven miles of underground limestone passages had been charted within the cave system in southwestern Georgia.

Decatur is the only county in the coastal plain of Georgia with underground limestone caverns. A few entries to Climax Caverns remain hidden. David had learned of one such opening from a cousin. His goal that day was to escape the heat and, he hoped, create a little of his own with DeeAnna. He started by dragging the cooler as far as the opening between the two rocks. Once he found a suitable private room in the limestone caverns, he'd go back for the sleeping bags to spread out like a picnic blanket. The bottoms of the sleeping bags were waterproof.

All he needed was for the flashlight batteries to hold their charge.

The entry was narrow, and DeeAnna complained. Eventually, David led them into a cavern the size of a hotel lobby. The air was noticeably cool. He shone his flashlight around the limestone walls. Just beyond a jutting of vertical rock, the caverns continued in a series of rooms into the deeper recesses of the cave.

"Keep your flashlight pointed down," David said. "There's water here and there."

He didn't want DeeAnna to point her flashlight straight up, in case bats were hanging from the ceiling. DeeAnna held his hand.

His cousin had told him of a small room-sized cavern off to the right with a skeleton in it. He told David to avoid that room, that it would give DeeAnna the creeps. He would recognize it, his cousin said, because an old wooden bed frame was in that room.

David's cousin thought the bed was from the War Between the States. It wasn't. It was much older.

DeeAnna saw the cat before David did. The cat walked a ledge just two feet or so from the cavern floor. DeeAnna screeched and dropped her flashlight. She wrapped her arms around David from behind.

"Over there," she said.

The cat's eyes lit up as David moved the beam of the flashlight. She was a funny-looking thing. Her fur was spiky. At first sight, it looked as though the cat had extra sets of ears, but it was just her fur sticking up in pointy locks. The cat's fur glistened like ice in the circle of yellow light from David's flashlight.

The cat walked the ledge slowly, watching the visitors to her cavern. She bounded away into the darkness. David tried to keep her in the light, but she quickly disappeared around a corner of rock.

"It's just a cat," he said. His voice echoed in the limestone chamber.

"I know that, David. I know what a cat is." She let go of him. It had felt warm and comfortable with her arms around him. It was cool in the cave. Cool enough for goose bumps. "It looked sort of strange, though."

"Just a cat," he said. "I think the place for our picnic is around that corner. See how the floor of the cave rises? It will be dry up that way."

"I think that cat wanted to show us something." DeeAnna retrieved her flashlight.

David rolled his eyes in the darkness. Whoever heard of a picnic cat?

They came to an elevated cavern and stood side by side looking at an old bed against the wall. David put his arm around DeeAnna. They both had their flashlights on the cat.

The bed was made. The spiky cat was curled on it, near the foot of a lace coverlet. She meowed once and waited. An antique doll lay on a down-stuffed pillow at the head of the bed. DeeAnna was drawn to it. She didn't see the little girl lying in bed next to her doll.

David did. He saw the girl as plain as day. She wore a long white gown that covered her legs and feet. Her hands were crossed on her chest. Her face was yellow and splotched. The splotches looked like leeches to David. They were open sores filled with dried blood. Downward smears of fresh blood were at both corners of her closed mouth. Her lips were blue. The little girl's eyes were swollen shut. Her hair rested loose around her head in a halo of yellow. It had slipped free from her scalp some time ago.

DeeAnna walked slowly toward the bed, mesmerized by the doll. She didn't see the girl at all. As DeeAnna reached for the doll, David saw the little girl's eyes open. Her eyes were black. Her eyes were empty holes in her stained and swollen face.

David screamed like ice water had been dumped on him in a hot shower.

He dropped his flashlight, and it broke. The spiky cat leapt off the bed and rushed out of the small chamber. David felt her dart by him like a blast of cold air.

DeeAnna screamed when David did. She turned quickly around, shining her flashlight on him. His mouth was open, but he couldn't speak. He tried to point behind DeeAnna.

"You scared me!" she yelled at him, having caught her breath.

DeeAnna turned her flashlight on the doll once more.

"Let's go," David said quietly. His pulse hammered. He drew a deep breath.

DeeAnna reached for the doll again.

"Now!" he shouted.

His voice echoed throughout the cave. He rushed forward and grabbed DeeAnna's arm. He wanted the flashlight and soon had it, but not before DeeAnna snatched up the doll for her own.

David kept the flashlight pointed toward the exit. His girlfriend's free hand in his, he pulled her from the bedside. Struggling not to slip on the wet chamber floors, David and DeeAnna hurried through the caverns. Warm sunlight streamed inside the cave in a horizontal shaft at the opening to the outside world, the opening to the safety of heat.

David dropped the flashlight and pushed DeeAnna outside ahead of him. She sat on the ice cooler, holding the doll in both hands, studying it.

"What was that room?" she said. "It looked like a movie set."

David Hyatt knew what the room was. He knew exactly. He didn't know whether or not he should tell DeeAnna.

"We have to go back, David. We have to take pictures of that."

"I'm never going back," he said.

"Why, are you afraid of the cat?"

"The cat's not real. It was just something . . . something we saw. The cat's not real."

"Okay, then. If you say so." She made a face, then laughed.

The little doll *was* real, and DeeAnna loved it. She'd never seen a doll this old. DeeAnna named her Sadie. Sadie's head was wooden and delicately painted. Her face was as new as the day she had been made. She wore a wig of perfectly arranged human hair. Her body was made of cloth, with soft kid leather arms and hands. Her dress was thin muslin embroidered with silk in yellow scrolls and red flowers, the sleeves and hem bordered with ribbon. There wasn't a worn spot or a tear anywhere.

DeeAnna thought the doll might date to the War Between the States, that it might have been hidden in the cave by its original owner during Sherman's March to the Sea.

Sadie was older than that.

The day was already hot, of course. It was July in Georgia. David struggled dragging the ice cooler back to the truck. He soaked his shirt through with sweat. Sweat ran down the backs of his legs inside his pants. DeeAnna walked casually behind, carrying her doll in both hands in front of her so she could look at it.

"Did you do that, David? Did you put Sadie there for me, then make me find her myself? Was that your mother's covers on the bed? You better go back and get them."

"No," was all he said.

David heard the spiky cat's meow and they neared his truck. The cat was following them. DeeAnna didn't seem to notice.

"Did you think I was going to get in that bed with you, David Hyatt? For a doll?"

"No."

"You just wanted me to have it, then? As a gift? Was it your grandmother's, or your great-grandma's? Is Sadie a member of your family, David?"

"No."

He unlocked and opened the passenger door for DeeAnna. She climbed in with Sadie. He left the door open for her until he had the air conditioning running. Sweat poured from his forehead as he lifted the cooler into the back. He wedged the sleeping bags around it. David started the truck, turned the air conditioner on high, then got out to walk around and close DeeAnna's door.

She smiled up at him.

When David was back in the driver's seat, he noticed that DeeAnna didn't look as if she were warm at all. His face was flushed. Hers wasn't. He was covered in sweat. Her sleeveless cotton blouse was as crisp and fresh as when she'd put it on that morning, not a spot of dampness anywhere. David closed the driver's door and drove away slowly on the rural lane. Dee-Anna left the doll in her lap. She leaned forward and turned the air conditioner down to low, then leaned toward David and kissed him on the cheek.

Her lips were cold.

"Thank you," she said. "I just love her. She's Sadie now."

She rested her hand on his leg. It felt to David as if someone had set a can of cold beer there.

He watched her carefully as he drove. DeeAnna looked only at her doll. Soon, she turned the air conditioning off altogether.

Sweat filled David's eyebrows. He rolled his window down. He was sweating through his shirt again. His back stuck to the seat.

DeeAnna was singing some sort of soft lullaby to the doll in a high little girl's voice. David couldn't make out the words. He noticed DeeAnna's legs had goose bumps.

She put her hand on David's shoulder. It felt like he had been touched with ice.

"We better go home now," she said.

Suddenly, DeeAnna's teeth were chattering. Her lips were pale. Her cheeks flushed red.

Ice, he thought. The cat had looked spiky because she was coated with ice.

"DeeAnna, listen to me," he said sternly. "Did you touch the cat?"

"She touched me, Daddy," DeeAnna said. "She's my kitty. I hug her when I want to. You gave her to me, Daddy."

David braked the pickup truck and brought it to a stop. He hopped out and ran around the front to DeeAnna's side. It was the doll. He opened her door and grabbed the doll from her and in one move threw it behind him. DeeAnna started crying.

He closed the door. As they drove away, DeeAnna seemed normal again. She stopped crying. She sat up and rubbed her arms, then her legs. She said that she was very, very cold.

David turned the heater on full blast. The cab of the truck was an oven. Sweat drenched his face and neck. It was July in Georgia, and he had the heater on. The tops of his hands were wet. The steering wheel was slick under his palms. His clothes were plastered with sweat.

"I'm freezing," DeeAnna said. "I'm colder than the dead."

Bright sunshine bounced off the hood of the truck. The pavement was hot enough to melt.

"You're cold because you have a fever," he said. "You need to go to bed, DeeAnna. You'll be warm soon."

David looked at her one last time, trying to decide whether to speed up or slow down. A thin glaze of ice coated DeeAnna's upper lip just under her nose. Her breath had frozen as it exited her mouth. Her nose was red.

He stopped the Toyota pickup again and hurried around to her side. DeeAnna was bent far forward in the seat. She clutched her sides in both arms, her teeth chattering.

David pulled her from the truck. He put his arm around her and forced her to walk. She felt like ice.

DeeAnna tried to stamp her feet when he told her to, but she couldn't feel them. Her feet were numb.

He brought her to the back of the truck, where he opened

the tailgate and told her to sit there. David clambered onto the bed liner and opened one of the quilted sleeping bags. He helped DeeAnna into the bag and zipped it up to her chin. Her cheeks and nose were white. It looked like frostbite. Drops of his sweat soaked into the sleeping bag.

David drove to the hospital.

The attendants left DeeAnna in the sleeping bag and rushed her inside on a gurney. One of the wheels fluttered. David trotted behind. A nurse inside the door told him to stop and have a seat in the emergency room waiting area.

Ten minutes later, a doctor came out and told David that DeeAnna was dead.

"I need to call her folks," David said, remembering how DeeAnna's hair had looked when they wheeled her in. Her hair was matted and spiky. It had looked varnished, like the cat's.

"Did she fall in water?" the doctor asked.

David Hyatt shook his head.

"She died of hypothermia," the doctor said. "Were you kids fooling around with a bathtub full of ice?"

"I think she had a fever," David said.

But he wasn't thinking about DeeAnna. He was thinking about the inner chamber in the caverns where a little girl with yellow hair had been quarantined long ago, before the War Between the States. It must have been a fever. A contagion. Her family had brought her bed in for her. They probably lit the room with candles. They must have brought her food and water. After all, they left the girl with her pet cat and her doll. It would have been summer. The limestone caverns would have been a cool respite from the cruel heat of Georgia in the summertime. The little girl was loved.

That night many years later on a country road in Decatur County, Georgia, a few people in cars might have noticed a pair of cat's eyes reflected in the headlights, a pair of glowing eyes moving along the roadside. They likely didn't see the antique doll in the spiky cat's mouth as she hurried through the stifling heat of July to return a cherished companion to its proper place within the cool limestone walls of a chamber far back in an uncharted area of Climax Caverns.

The faithful cat, still unprepared to say goodbye to her charge, was doing everything she possibly could in the afterlife to keep the little girl cool and content.

Cat Cookies

≈ ≈ ≈ ≈ ≈ ≈ ≈ ≈ ≈ ≈ ≈ ≈ ≈ ≈

All the kids in the mountain town of Sylva, North Carolina, knew the best place to go on Halloween. Wearing their
costumes, they rode their bicycles from Main up Walnut or
Spring, across Jackson to the Camden shortcut, then to winding Ridgeway Drive. They left before dark. Some years, it
looked like a regular parade. Some years, it looked like a race.

Small children on the backs of bicycles or riding on the
handlebars held on tightly to their masks, their fairy princess
wands, their construction-paper witches' hats. They clutched
orange plastic jack-o'-lanterns and decorated brown paper
sacks to their chests.

They were going to Laura Peasy's place. Even when it rained
on Halloween, they rode their bikes to Laura Peasy's first. The

children stopped at many other houses for trick or treat before the evening was through. But not until they were on their way back from Laura Peasy's. Every fourth-grader knew you went to the best place first, before the treats ran out.

No kid in Sylva wanted to arrive at Laura Peasy's house on Halloween once she had turned out the lights and left nothing but a few leftover apples on the porch steps. No one wanted to be at Laura Peasy's any other night, for that matter, after the lights were out. Her yard was full of cats, and the cats were scary in the dark.

Some adults in Sylva dressed up in costumes for Halloween. Laura didn't need to. She was a witch, and real witches dressed the way everyone else did. It's been that way forever in the Smoky Mountains.

Sylva is a picturesque county seat of about 2,500 people. The charming railroad town is nestled in a small valley among the rising, lush green hills of the Smoky Mountains. Elevations in heavily forested Jackson County rise dramatically from Sylva's 2,050 feet to lofty perches at 6,450 feet. The Nantahala National Forest covers more than 28,000 acres of the county. The Jackson County Courthouse, with its large clock tower under a green copper dome, stands atop a hill at the west end of Main Street in Sylva, overlooking the small downtown of brick storefronts and shops and the railroad along Mill Street.

Almost everyone in Sylva knew the number of steps up the hill to the courthouse. So did Laura Peasy. She counted them when she registered at the courthouse for citizenship. And she counted them going down again.

Laura's older sister, Olivia, fell in love with an American

soldier stationed in England during World War II. They married. Laura moved with Olivia and her new husband to Sylva at the end of the war. The young soldier was a stonemason. The first job he undertook upon his return from war was to build a stone cottage in a small mountain cove off the ridge road overlooking his western North Carolina hometown.

The stone house of Laura and the newlyweds had five rooms, including the bathroom. It had nine windows, two doors, and a stone fireplace. The fireplace was special. The soldier used his best stones and cleverly configured the letter *V* in the outside stonework just above the roofline. The *V* was for *Victory*. He laid it out in smooth stones and painted them white.

For years, locals referred to the stone cottage as "Victory House," but it's not called that by many anymore. The white paint washed off the stones after the soldier died. He was buried in the front yard of the cottage, at his own request, under an arch of carefully cut stones he took from the ridge next to the house. He'd created similar arched monuments and headstones for Olivia and Laura as well.

"You can see me from the front porch when my day comes," he told his wife. "And I can see you."

During the early years following the war, Laura became the cook of the household. She was afraid of snakes and preferred staying indoors. The mountains around Sylva had more snakes than all of the British Isles combined, she was sure. With maybe India thrown in. She'd seen one the first day she moved there. She saw another in the creek. There were snakes by the wellhouse. They were everywhere.

Laura became an excellent baker using the wood-burning

oven, which she believed was more uniformly hot than electric ones. The bread and rolls, the cakes and pies, the cookies she placed in the iron oven baked evenly from all sides at once. Baked goods, especially breads, were best cooked in that manner.

People traveling the ridge road while Laura was baking became hungry without quite knowing why. The smell of her baked goods filled the mountain air, hung close to the ground with the fog, circled the trees, drifted in fingers of subtle aroma across the road. The fingers tickled your nose, and your stomach, too.

Animals smelled something cooking. The neighbors' braying hounds kept the bears away. But stray cats looking for a handout were clever enough, or hungry enough, to slip by a few roaming dogs and find their way to Laura's house. Laura adopted any cat that came along. Cats, she knew, kept the snakes away.

When Olivia's husband fell and crippled his back, Olivia took care of him. She also chopped firewood, maintained the garden and the small orchard, and did the laundry. Laura began to take her baked goods to town. She learned to drive the farm truck, the one with the missing passenger-side door. Before she drove the truck in the morning, Laura put one of the cats into the cab to search for snakes. Laura poked under the seats with a long stick. When she got the truck started, the cat trotted back to the stone porch, its job done for the day, at least until it had a mouse to catch.

Laura bartered freshly baked loaves of bread at the two grocery stores for eggs and milk, flour and sugar. She sold cinnamon rolls, honey buns, fruit pies, and specialty cakes to the restaurants and the hotel for cash money. Her eagerly sought breads sold out the day she brought them in, usually before noon. Cheese bread was one of the favorites. No one was certain how she made it work. The homemade bread tasted so lightly of cheese that you had to have another piece to be sure. She baked a cucumber bread, too. It sold out next.

Still, it was her rose-and-orange bread that made Laura famous. She baked the bread one year as a Christmas treat, just to see if she could. Laura soon found she was making it year-round, as it quickly became the most desired bread in town. It sold for fifty cents more a loaf than the others. The bread baked reddish pink in the middle and was tinted toward orange at the outside edges.

The recipe was Laura's own. She got the idea from a cat that lived on her porch, an adopted stray. It was a light orange cat with a pink nose that looked exactly, Laura thought, like a rose. She wanted to make a bread those pastel colors exactly. Laura managed it with a mortar and pestle, a bit of orange zest in one dough, a quarter-drop of rose oil from the pharmacy in the other. And one rose petal for each loaf, like a nose for a cat.

The bread tasted of orange and so faintly of rose that a single bite held in your mouth was said to taste exactly like a slice of summer. Some said it tasted like a kiss. No wedding reception in Sylva or anywhere else in Jackson County was considered complete without a tray of cut slices of Laura Peasy's rose-and-orange bread. The secret was to make two separate doughs and fashion them in a bread pan just so. Of course, the oven had to be hot or the doughs would blend and come out tan.

Laura bought baking pans at the hardware store and sold small loaves of bread individually to railway passengers in Sylva. They let her on the train at one end of town and dropped her off at the other. The trainmen loved her bread as much as anyone.

She baked in that wood stove every morning, afternoon, and night. Even when she drove into town, a patch of fog riding in the passenger seat thanks to the missing door, the stove was kept hot.

When Olivia died, Laura had her older sister buried in her proper place. Laura didn't like looking at the three monuments, especially the one made for her. She allowed the arched stonework to become overgrown with rhododendron and thorny vines.

Laura missed her sister, but she had her oven to keep her company those last several years. And she had her cats. Laura loved baking. Laura loved cats. And she loved Halloween more than any other time of the year. Halloween was the best part of living in America. It was her opportunity to contribute to the town, to make children happy.

By the end of summer, the cats began stacking up at the stone cottage off the ridge road above Sylva. As everyone knew who provided homes for God's stray pets, cats multiplied in spring and summer. By the time the leaves turned, there were too many for the porch. The new cats wanted their own homes. They wanted forever homes, where they could be the cats in charge, instead of being eighth or ninth at the end of a row of cats on the porch.

At Halloween, the children came to Laura Peasy's house. She wanted them all to come to the stone cottage, as many children as the road would hold. For the magic, ghostly night of trick or treat, Laura went all out. She made popcorn balls in three different colors. She made caramel apples and cinnamon apples on sticks. She baked thick sugar cookies cut into the shapes of Halloween.

She baked witch cookies and pumpkin cookies decorated with jack-o'-lantern faces. Ghost-shaped cookies. She had a scarecrow cookie, too. For the older boys, Laura made cookies in the shapes of spiders and flying bats.

The old witches in England cast spells by boiling eggs. Laura made cat-shaped cookies, the cats both sitting and standing up. Laura had twenty-seven colors of frosting with which to decorate the cookies. The cat cookies all had whiskers, and the correct colors for fur and eyes.

Laura made a small sack of goodies for each child who came to her door on Halloween.

≈ ≈ ≈ ≈

"You have to do something, you know," Henry Williston said, leaning his bicycle against a shrub along the pathway to Laura Peasy's house.

Henry was eleven. He was dressed as a pirate. His long underwear sported tattoos in black felt marker. A skull and crossbones were on his chest. He wore a magic-marker mustache.

"Like what?" Paula Andrews asked.

She was his nine-year-old neighbor. Paula hadn't been to Laura's before. Henry's mother made him take her along.

"Sing or dance or tell a story." Henry adjusted his father's necktie, which was tied around his head like a bandanna. "If she likes what you do, you get a special bag of treats. She has them done up in advance."

Paula didn't know a song she could sing to a stranger except the one she'd learned for the Christmas program at church. She was dressed as a fairy princess, and she worried that a fairy princess wouldn't ever sing a Christmas song. She wore her jeans under a red felt skirt decorated with glitter. She carried a magic wand of aluminum foil wrapped over a cardboard star on a stick. Paula liked Halloween because she was allowed to wear her mother's lipstick and have rouge on her cheeks. Maybe she could tell the lady she was an angel.

The only other song she knew was "Ruby, Don't Take Your Love to Town," because it was on the radio. And she knew only part of it.

"Maybe just answer questions," Henry said. "If you get them right, you get the special treats. They're like the other treats, except you get one of each, and something added to that."

Laura's little brown bags of treats were special indeed. This year, she had six of them. Each one contained a cat cookie that matched one of her porch cats that needed a home. Even the whiskers were the right colors. She mixed her icing colors like Michelangelo mixed paints.

"Here," Henry said, "hand me the flashlight and hold my hand. You go first."

"Oh, my," Laura said when she answered the door. "You must be a fairy princess with a magic wand!"

A cat from the porch walked to Paula and rubbed against her jeans. It sat and looked up at her glittering skirt, then watched the aluminum-foil stick in her hand. Paula leaned down and petted the cat with her free hand, trying all the time to see around Laura, to see what things were in her house.

"Do you have a kitty at home, dear?"

Paula shook her head.

"I only know one song," the little girl said.

The cat walked around her feet and rubbed the other leg. Henry took a step backward on the stone porch.

"You are Sarah Andrews's girl, I bet. I knew your mother when she was your age. She looked just like you."

Paula took a deep breath. The song, "Silent Night," was a hard one. Paula started it, holding her magic wand and moving it with each syllable. The cat sat at her feet and stared straight up, its head moving with the aluminum-foil star.

Laura Peasy held a finger to her lips. "Here, I have something for you." The old lady stepped back into the house and handed Paula one of the brown paper lunch sacks. "Trick or treat, dear," Laura said.

"Trick or treat," Paula said.

"Now, honey, that cookie on top is just for you. You eat that one yourself and don't give it to anybody else."

Paula Andrews nodded and turned away with her prize. Other kids were lining up in the yard, waiting their turns on the porch.

"And you must be a buccaneer from a pirate ship," Laura said to Henry, who turned his flashlight on and pointed it at his face. Five cats watched Henry without moving. Laura always let the cats decide. Henry picked out two popcorn balls for his treat.

A cat the color of the special cookie in Paula's bag followed her home that night. Though it was a long trot for a cat, the route from Ridgeway Drive was mostly downhill. Paula's mother said she could keep the cat, but she had to take care of it herself.

≈ ≈ ≈ ≈

There are 107 steps to the Jackson County Courthouse, 108 if you count the last one. People in Sylva say that's how many cats Laura Peasy found homes for before she died. Before the little stone house fell into ruin.

Everyone in Sylva knows the number of steps up the hill to the courthouse, just as everyone knows that Laura Peasy was always a witch at baking, and that she always made her cookies from scratch.

Chimney Cats

≈ ≈ ≈ ≈ ≈ ≈ ≈ ≈ ≈ ≈ ≈ ≈ ≈

Charles had lived in Savannah all his life. When he married Nancy, they moved into a two-story Victorian in the historic River Street district. The former owners had painted the front door red. The house was famous for its brick chimneys, but Charles was not aware of that when they moved in.

When their son, Brandon, was four years old, he started hearing noises on the roof at night and didn't want to sleep in the upstairs bedroom across the hall from Charles and Nancy's. They told him the sounds were baby doves and roof rabbits. They were nothing bad and wouldn't hurt anyone. They helped keep the house warm at night.

The next evening, Brandon came into their room crying. He said he was afraid the bunnies were going to fall off the roof and die.

Nancy told him that roof rabbits were a very special type of bunny that couldn't fall off anything. And if they did fall, she told him, roof rabbits would drift softly down like cotton balls, then bounce right back up to their place on the roof.

"Next, he's going to be afraid of cotton," Charles said, once Brandon have finally gone back to sleep.

"You mean like you're afraid of taking out the trash at night?" Nancy said.

Charles made a face.

It wasn't cotton that Brandon was afraid of next. It was the bedroom fireplace. He screamed at the fireplace one night when he was six.

Brandon wet the bed that night. Charles and Nancy found him crying. He was shaking from head to toe, pointing at the little brick fireplace. Nancy carried him from the room and cleaned him up. Charles stripped the sheets from the bed.

"He won't remember it in the morning," Charles predicted.

Brandon remembered it. He said he saw long, furry animals coming out of the fireplace and shooting across the floor like racecars. The six-year-old said they had glowing eyes and made motor sounds.

Nancy talked it over with Charles. "Maybe it was a squirrel or something," she suggested.

"The chimneys are screened. He's just imagining it."

"We don't use the bedroom fireplaces anyway," she said. "Maybe we could have Brandon's bricked over. It will still look nice if we paint the bricks."

Charles purchased a cast-iron fireplace cover at a local antique shop and had it bolted into place. The iron plate featured a high-relief image of flowers in a basket. Nancy painted the basket light blue and the flowers white. Charles kept his fingers crossed that his son would find nothing in the flowers to be afraid of in the middle of the night.

By the time Brandon was ten, he was over his night terrors. In early October, he informed his father that he wanted to go on one of the ghost tours of Savannah. All the kids in his class at school were doing it.

But Charles wasn't convinced that a ghost tour was a good idea just yet.

"Maybe when he's twelve," Charles told Nancy. "The stories are all butchery and bloody murder. Anyplace anyone in Savannah experienced a violent death, they say a ghost lives there."

"He's hearing the stories at school anyway. It doesn't seem to do him any harm. Boys his age love that sort of thing."

"I looked it up on the Internet. Savannah has thirty-one different ghost tours. You can go on one ghost tour every day for an entire month."

"Is that official?" she teased. "Did you use the calculator?"

"Okay, have your fun. In 2002, the American Institute of Parapsychology recognized Savannah as American's Most Haunted City."

"And they don't even know about the roof rabbits," she said.

"But get this, every single ghost tour includes the Colonial Park Cemetery."

"And?"

"Who wants to walk around a cemetery and listen to ghost stories? It's disrespectful, Nancy, to talk about ghosts

in front of the dead. Good people are buried there. Somebody's relatives."

"You're afraid of graveyards, Charles! You're the one, not
Brandon. You're just a scaredy-cat, is what you are."

He gave in. "Well, he wants to go at night. He says the
daytime tours aren't the good ones. So it will be at night, if you
don't mind taking him."

"Charles! I will not. Shame on you."

"What?"

"No boy Brandon's age wants to go on a ghost tour with
his mother. He'd be embarrassed. What if the boys at school
found out?"

Charles selected a tour that started in the early evening,
one that drove by the Colonial Park Cemetery but didn't stop
there for a casual stroll among the rotting bones. Only one portion of this tour was a brief walkabout. The remaining ghost
stories were told on the tour bus, so the haunted delights of
old Savannah would be enjoyed through the windows. It was
nearly perfect for a ghost tour, and one that Brandon eagerly
agreed would be lots of fun.

The October evening was cool. A moon hung over the old
port city. Nancy made hot cocoa and filled a thermos. Before
leaving, Charles laid a fire in the downstairs parlor. As always,
he experienced the strange sensation of someone or something
standing right behind him as he leaned forward to start the
fire. It never failed to raise the hair on the back of his neck. The
sensation went away as soon as he lit the fire.

It was the same sensation he had when he took the trash
out at night. He felt as if something were behind him on his

way back to the house, getting closer at every step. It was something much taller than a cat, something on two feet. Charles often broke into a run, rushing to the door of the house. His heart raced. If he didn't hurry, he would be caught. Someone, he felt, was chasing him, wanting him to linger in the night.

The overwhelming dread of being chased, of being caught, slowly evaporated as soon as he closed the door and stood once more safely inside his house. His heart rate returned to normal, and he felt silly about the whole thing. Most people were afraid of bears or bats or snakes. These were reasonable things to be frightened by. Charles was afraid of taking out the trash at night.

Nancy had caught him once. He was breathless and flushed. His pulse pounded. He had just closed the door behind him. She asked what happened. Charles must have looked as if something had.

"Do you believe in ghosts?" Charles wanted to know. He tried to ask the question casually. He even grinned a little.

"Why, Charles, do you think ghosts are in our yard?"

"Of course not," he said. He noticed that Nancy hadn't answered his question.

Charles never brought it up again. It was childish, he decided. Still, every time he lit a fire in the house, someone seemed to be standing behind him, ready to give him a push.

The night of the tour was no exception. He rose from the fireplace to tell Brandon it was time to go. As he walked across the room, Charles stumbled over something that wasn't there. It wasn't a slight stumble or a mere misstep. He tripped over something large and heavy and nearly fell. Nothing was there. It felt like a body as much as anything. That happened in the house from time to time. Charles had never mentioned it to anyone.

On the bus, Brandon listened intently. He sat next to the window with his hands folded in his lap. The tour was more interesting than Charles had anticipated. He recognized most of the buildings and houses.

The tour guide was young and spoke passionately of the history of Savannah.

"Ghosts may be dead people," he said, "but they are our living links to the past. Whenever someone experiences a ghost, that person is being touched by history. Though a ghost may feel cold to many, it is that icy touch that keeps the history of an individual warm and alive, if only for a moment. Ghosts are reminders that history is personal, that all things we call history were experienced in a different place or time by people. People just like us in so many ways."

Charles learned that most ghosts, the ones experienced over and over through the years, are the results of unhappy deaths or improper burials.

"Most ghosts have unresolved issues," the tour guide said. "Most ghosts want to be laid to rest. It is actually their desire to go away. A ghost of a person who was improperly buried cannot rest. So it stays."

Brandon also learned what his father had discovered on the Internet, that Savannah has more ghosts than most places.

"You can't count the number of ghosts in Savannah," the tour guide continued. "There are too many of them. It is said of this old port city that a ghost is under every tree."

Brandon asked his dad if he knew how many trees were in

Savannah. Charles smiled and shook his head.

The tour bus stopped alongside the Colonial Park Cemetery.

"There really shouldn't be too many ghosts in a cemetery," the guide said. "After all, these people all received proper burial. And their remains lie undisturbed, each in his or her own appropriate place. Sounds good, doesn't it?"

The guide paused, looking from face to face at the people on the bus.

"But not all burials are proper ones, even in a cemetery. Bodies of people without church affiliation, bodies of people without family, bodies of the unloved and the unwanted are sometimes hastily buried in cemeteries, at the back in unmarked graves. Over time, other bodies are added to existing graves.

"Women who were thought to be witches were buried face down in their graves. This was to keep them from returning and to have them pointed in the wrong direction, should they try. Murderers executed for their crimes were sometimes buried the same way. And because they deserved punishment beyond bodily death, because neither a murderer nor a witch should be allowed the luxury of eternal rest, colonial Americans would bury the worst of them face down under heavily traveled crossroads.

"From what we know of ghost lore and the history of the South, however, some people really do turn over in their graves. They slip out from under the heavy traffic of roadways and find their way, in moments of sheer terror for us, to touch the living with the icy cold fingers of their histories."

The guide informed them that in 1967 several bodies had

been unearthed in Savannah while roadwork was being done on Abercorn Street. "Right here," he said, "next to the Colonial Park Cemetery." The street and sidewalk had been laid out in 1896. No record existed of bodies being removed. Either the workers had taken away tombstones to lay a street atop existing graves or the street cut through a portion of the cemetery with unmarked graves, where the outcasts of Savannah society had been haphazardly interred.

"Some Savannah ghosts may simply be trying to tell us where they are buried," the young guide continued. British soldiers holding the port city in 1779 had come under heavy assault by colonial forces in what some historians say was the bloodiest hour of the American Revolution. While the British managed to repulse the attack, they suffered heavy losses.

"The dead from that battle alone numbered eleven hundred. Existing records note that the dead were buried in a mass grave within what is now the historic district of Savannah. The location of that grave has never been discovered. It is entirely unknown to us even today.

"The wheels of this bus may be upon that grave at any moment during tonight's tour. Every structure erected in Savannah after 1779 may have beneath its foundation a thousand or more ghosts."

Brandon asked his dad about their house. He wanted to know if it had been built before or after 1779. Charles didn't smile. He turned his palms up and shrugged, as if he didn't know.

After a few more streets, and following a brief discussion of the Great Fire of 1820 and a handful of yellow fever outbreaks, the tour came to a pause in a residential section of the River Street district. The group disembarked for a stroll among some of Savannah's oldest homes.

Charles and Brandon recognized the streets and most of the houses in their neighborhood. Even familiar things looked different at night. Especially tonight, a night filled with stories of ghosts.

The Savannah ghosts in this section of town had proper names. They were the names of former residents of some of the homes. An occupant had died. Someone decades later heard a noise in the attic or saw a light come on when no one was home, and, bingo, you had a ghost story for the tourist trade. Charles bet he could come up with a ghost for every house on his block. He hoped Brandon was mature enough to figure this out for himself.

Could there possibly be an old Savannah house where no former occupant had ever died? Now, that would be a story, Charles decided.

The group bustled down the street, listening to the tour guide's every word. He pointed here. Murder. He pointed there. Love triangle.

Then the group huddled in front of Charles's house.

"Breathe in," the guide instructed the group. He breathed in deeply, then breathed out.

Brandon breathed in with the rest of them. Charles wasn't so sure he needed to. The lights were on in the parlor. He wondered just how long a ghost tour had been stopping at his house. He couldn't wait to tell Nancy. Somehow, this was all her fault.

"Smell that?" the guide asked. "What you might be smelling is Isabel Tyler's cats."

What Charles believed he smelled was the drift of wood smoke from his own fireplace. That and the cologne of the little bald man standing next to him.

"Or," the guide continued, "what you might smell on the night air is the stench of suicide and burning fingers."

Some in the group nodded their heads and whispered to each other that, in fact, the smell of suicide might be in the air. Brandon beamed broadly at his dad. Charles saw that the boy couldn't wait to tell his friends that he lived in an official haunted house. Yes, this was all Nancy's fault.

"Quick!" the guide shouted. He pointed upward. "Look at the roof! Look to both sides of the chimney."

The guide wanted to know if anyone in the group saw cats.

"Shadows," a woman replied. "I saw shadows."

Charles wanted to tell her they were roof rabbits, not cats.

"I saw one," Brandon said.

"This time of year," the guide said, "people see cats there, near the chimney."

"Brandon," Charles said sternly, "you did not see a cat."

"Did so," Brandon said. "I knew they weren't rabbits, Dad. You and Mom just made that up."

"The current residents do not own cats," the guide explained. "They are afraid of cats."

"I am not!" Charles said.

Everyone in the group turned to look at Charles. Brandon smiled again.

"Yes, they are very afraid of cats," the guide said, mistaking Charles for an out-of-towner, a tourist. Charles quickly realized his mistake. He had no intention of introducing himself to the group, nor to the tour guide, for that matter. He didn't interrupt again. He didn't try to explain.

His house, Charles learned, was haunted by ghost cats. And by the victim of a lunatic suicide. Not to mention her fingers.

A woman named Isabel Tyler had committed suicide in the house in 1916. The Savannah man to whom she was engaged was killed in France in World War I.

Charles doubted that such a woman ever existed. He doubted that anyone named Tyler had ever owned the house, but he was uncertain one way or the other. Besides, people did commit suicide. It happened. Why would the house end up being haunted by cats?

The tour guide asked everyone to take another breath. Charles refused to participate.

"You might be able to catch a little whiff of Isabel herself," the guide said. "Her body lay in front of the fireplace for weeks. It was by smell alone that she was finally discovered. Before killing herself, Isabel Tyler became a total lunatic."

Brandon was beside himself with glee at hearing this. He bounced up and down in excitement. Charles considered suing the ghost tour. They couldn't go around saying that he was afraid of cats. They had no right to do that. It was slander to make up things about real people and then tell everyone.

"She lived alone in that house with two cats, and she went insane with grief," the guide said. "In the end, she couldn't face the town, her family, her fiancé's family. Isabel Tyler could not face life itself. You see, she was several months pregnant when she got the news her future husband had died. Isabel's fiancé had signed up and been shipped overseas as part of the Allied forces more than a year earlier. Neither could she show her face, and especially her pregnancy, at the funeral."

He paused.

"You know what they say in the South? 'Momma's baby, Papa's maybe.'"

The tour guide smiled briefly, as if waiting for applause, then continued.

"Oh, the citizens of Savannah knew all about that. And a married woman would never be asked about the parentage of her offspring, not in church and not on the street.

"You see, Isabel had lost all hope of ever being married in Savannah. She could confront her future husband with her shame, and it might not go well for her. But when he was killed on the battlefield, Isabel's only remaining hope was gone. She went insane over it.

"She cut off all her hair and burned it in the fireplace. Then she chopped off her own fingers with a hatchet and threw them in the fireplace, too."

Charles considered opening the gate and going home, making Brandon come with him. His car, though, was at the parking lot where the tour had begun. So he listened impatiently, tapping his foot on the sidewalk, while Brandon soaked in every word.

The guide's story ended soon enough. Apparently, Isabel had been so alone at the end that she wanted her cats in heaven with her. She killed them first and burned their bodies in the fireplace, right after she'd burned the hair from her head, and just before she cut off her fingers and tossed all ten in the fireplace. That's why the cat ghosts smelled of burning fur.

The odor was carried on the night air in Charles's Savannah neighborhood.

It was all a bunch of bunk. It was all made up, as far as Charles was concerned. If she cut off her fingers, how could she throw them in the fireplace? She would have had to push them in with her feet. He was surprised the story didn't have her dancing pregnant and naked with the devil on the chimney top.

An old man in the tour group approached Charles when the story was over. They were walking back to the bus. The old man grabbed Charles's arm to slow him down.

"Yes?" Charles said. There was one in every group, an old geezer still dressing up in clothes from his wedding. This one wore a suit and tie right out of the 1930s. His eyes looked glassy, as old eyes sometimes do.

"I'm from here, too," the old man said. "This tour doesn't have it right, you know? I've been to that house before, when the front door was painted blue."

The old man nodded back toward Charles's house.

"Cats took her fingers. Nobody cuts off their own fingers. Not both hands."

"I see," Charles said. The guy was a queer old coot, but he said the same thing Charles had been thinking all along. If you cut the fingers off one hand, what hand would you use to cut off the remaining fingers?

"Those cats are voodoo haints," the old man said. "They're looking for the baby to take back. The next baby. They'll wait till there's one. They've waited this long."

Moonlight fell between the trees, turning the old man's white hair into a soft glow. His lips looked red in the moonlight, as if he wore lipstick, and his sunken cheeks looked rouged. As the man turned, a sparkle of light glistened at his lapel. A polished gold wedding band was pinned there. *That's different*, Charles thought.

"Izzy, now she was pregnant, all right. But she did the wrong thing when her man died in France. She was grieving, but she did the wrong thing. Izzy sought out a voodoo granny to come to the house. She wanted to get rid of the baby. She wasn't as far along as that fellow said she was."

"Is that so?" Charles said. He wondered why an old man would be wearing makeup. Brandon walked next to them, listening.

"That's the way things were then. Only that voodoo granny was smart. She didn't do what Izzy wanted. She pretended to, and then when it was too late she arranged to take Izzy's baby for her and find it a home. Things were done in the house back in those days. Izzy could stay in the house the whole last part of when that baby was growing inside her. No one would see. And she could give it to the voodoo woman, who wouldn't tell anyone a thing about it. They made an agreement, those two."

They'd stopped walking. Charles didn't know what to believe, but the story concerned his house, so he wanted to listen.

"Izzy had a change of heart. She found someone she could trust. It was her father-in-law—well, the man who was to be—and he would see that a better home was found for the child than what the voodoo witch had in mind. He got a midwife from out of town for Izzy, too. So, when the baby came, Izzy didn't call for the voodoo granny. That baby of hers went elsewhere."

Charles told his son to get on the bus. Brandon shouldn't be hearing this. Reluctantly, the boy did as he was told.

"Fine boy you have there," the old man said.

Charles nodded. "What about the cats?"

"Well, they're voodoo haints. Those aren't normal cats. They're agents for that granny woman. She sent them around to collect her due. Those old swamp women use cats to do their voodoo, for sure they do. What you have to do to keep them out for good is paint your doors blue. Light blue, you know? Voodoo haints can't cross blue. They think it's water. And they don't know how deep it is, so they just won't go that way. Not ever."

Charles remembered having heard this before. When he was a boy, he'd heard it.

"And poor Izzy didn't commit suicide. That fellow had it wrong. She was killed by those cats. They showed up to collect the old granny's baby and ended up bringing Izzy's fingers back. That's all they got from Isabel Tyler.

"Those cats being there drove her crazy. Maybe they killed her. They got behind her and pushed her in the fireplace while it was burning. Or maybe they tripped her and she fell that way. It's her hair you smell in the neighborhood when a fire's going. Her hair, not the cats'. Then they took her fingers. Once they're sent to get something, voodoo cats can't come back empty-handed."

"What about the cats now?" Charles asked.

The cats were still there.

"Well, sir, I've been meaning to say this to you for some time now."

In the moonlight, the old man's lips looked dry. They

looked like they would fall off his face if he spoke too loudly.

"When you come out of the house at night, that's me waiting to talk to you. Those folks in the house ahead of you painted the door red. They didn't stay in your house very long at all, before they up and moved. You and your lady should go back and paint the door blue. Those cat haints will go elsewhere."

Charles joined the stragglers getting on the bus. The old man's words slid by like the breeze. Sitting next to Brandon, he understood what the man had said about trying to talk to him before. The bus lurched forward. The guide would be talking soon.

"Don't believe a word of it," Charles told his son. "Not a word about our house is true."

"We have to tell Mom, don't we?"

"I don't know, Brandon, if it would be the sort of thing she needs to hear. There's more cocoa, if you want some."

Charles asked his son where the old man was sitting on the bus. He wanted to talk to the old man about what he'd said concerning his trying to talk to Charles when he came out of the house at night. It would have been the nights Charles carried out the trash.

"He didn't get on with us," Brandon said. "He wasn't on the bus to begin with. He just sort of showed up. Did you notice his feet?"

"His feet?"

"Yeah, Dad. Didn't you see his feet? He wasn't wearing any shoes."

Charles didn't remember. But he did recall that this was the night before trash pickup.

Maybe he would set the alarm early and take the trash out

before the trucks got started in the morning. It would be light then. And the cats would be off the roof. Charles had seen them both when the guide told the group to look at the chimney of his house earlier that night.

He'd stop by the hardware store on his way to work. He'd buy a can or two of blue paint.

Butcher Cat

~ ~ ~ ~ ~ ~ ~ ~ ~ ~ ~ ~ ~ ~ ~

Jessica Prewitt was mean enough to throw rocks at you. And she taught Sunday school at Larry Crawford's church in Tuscaloosa, Alabama. It didn't seem right to Larry.

Until he was old enough to have a car, Larry walked to school every day in Tuscaloosa. It was how he first met Jessica Prewitt and learned how mean she was at heart. She was mean to everyone.

For bad weather and on cold days, Larry knew a shortcut to school. He crossed the cemetery. The cemetery was on his way, and it was too big to walk all the way around twice a day, especially when it rained.

He always hurried through the cemetery. It wasn't that dead people scared him, although that was reason enough not

162   Butcher Cat

to dawdle. He hurried through the cemetery at a jog because of that mean old lady Jessica Prewitt. Larry worried about Finger Man and Butcher Cat at night, when he walked home from football and basketball games. At night in the graveyard, it was difficult not to think about the story that Jessica told the boys in Sunday school.

Finger Man and Butcher Cat showed up together in the cemetery, according to Jessica. And they were what you had to watch out for at night. You had to watch out for both of them, but particularly the cat.

During the day, Larry kept an eye out for Jessica herself. She wasn't supposed to, but she gardened in the old part of the cemetery, where no grave markers were left intact. Just a few broken stones. She planted strawberries all around those graves. Jessica lived in a small house across the road from the cemetery. Jessica's house was easy to pick out by the scarecrow she kept out front.

Jessica herself was scarier. She lost her mind when kids walked through her graveyard strawberries, or when they looked as if they might be going to. She threw rocks. She ran after Jackie Mills, Jr., with a shovel in her hand once when she caught him crossing the cemetery on his way home from school. He had to circle the marble angel in the middle of the cemetery to get away from her. When she didn't have garden weaponry nearby, Jessica would jump out from behind a tree, snarling like a dog, and chase you with her bare hands. Usually, she threw rocks.

Jessica was too mean to teach Sunday school, but she did.

In Larry Crawford's class at church, she told the boys the story of Finger Man and Butcher Cat, sparing no gruesome detail. They lived in the cemetery now, she informed them. Now and forever. A butcher cat is a cat trained to distract a farm animal when it is about to be slaughtered. It paces back and forth in front of the cow, and stands on its hind legs and paws the air. The butcher cat meows like it's talking. The cow lowers her head for a closer look, and when she is fully distracted the butcher kills the cow.

"Butcher Cat is in the cemetery now," Jessica said. "God keeps him there for the likes of you. For the likes of people who would trample graves with no purpose."

When you see Butcher Cat, the boys learned, it's too late. Because Butcher Cat always comes along with Finger Man.

"Butcher Cat will show up in front of you just like that!" she said. "You think that cat came from somewhere, but it just shows up. It paces back and forth to get your attention, boys. It meows to beat the band. It will stand on its hind legs and paw the air. Anything to get you to look."

As soon as someone looked, it was too late to save them. Finger Man was already standing behind the person. He would stick a boy in the back with his long, sharp finger of pure bone.

"Right in the spine," Jessica said. "You're done for, boys. You can't move a muscle. That finger bone holds you like a nail in the cross of Jesus."

Larry guessed her story had something to do with Sunday school after all. He didn't like the way Jessica's mouth moved when she talked. There was spit in the corners where her lips met. She was drooling over her story, drooling like a dog when you're about to feed it supper.

"All Finger Man has is bones, you see. He wears a long

coat and a hat to cover it up as well as he can. But all he has is bones. And he wants flesh, boys. He wants your flesh. He takes your fingers first, because his are all bone. He reaches around and takes them off your hand. Jerks them clean off, five at a time. If you try to holler and scream for help, or say anything, that's when he reaches around with his other hand and pulls out your tongue."

According to Jessica, once Finger Man pulled the tongue out of your mouth, he threw it to the cat.

"Just like a butcher does. That's when the bleeding starts, boys. That's when it starts hurting the most. He takes all your skin and all your blood. Finger Man puts your eyeballs in his hat. He takes everything until there's nothing left of you. Best stay out of the cemetery, day or night. Best stay clean away, lest you see Butcher Cat. And then it's too late. Once you look, you're gone!"

Larry asked his mom why they let that crazy old lady teach Sunday school anyway.

"She's a God-fearing woman. You let her be. She's old now and lives alone, and she's scared of boys like you. You're too rambunctious. She's scared of you. So you just let her be. Don't you dare be bothering her none."

"Yes, ma'am."

When Larry Crawford graduated high school, he joined the navy and went to sea. He told the story of Butcher Cat to everybody on his ship at one time or another. He told about Butcher Cat and Finger Man in the cemetery in Tuscaloosa. Everyone liked it. They wanted to know, though, how the story ended, whether or not Larry or anyone he knew had actually seen the cat in the cemetery.

"No," he would tell them. "It ends when you see that cat. The story ends right there."

Larry came home the next October to see his family and visit friends. Jessica Prewitt had gotten meaner while he was gone. She was in the cemetery all day. She had a slingshot now and would fire off rocks at kids cutting through too close to her strawberry patch. She was there in the morning and the evening, waiting for anybody cutting through.

"The police have talked to her once or twice," Larry's mother said. "But there's nothing they can do. She's senile now. It happens to old people."

Larry believed Jessica Prewitt had been senile all along.

"Don't you dare be mean to her, you hear? She was a good woman most of her life, you remember that. Don't you bother her none."

"Yes, ma'am." Larry wasn't about to bother Jessica Prewitt.

"It's Halloween time, and you know how boys like to go into that cemetery on Halloween. She put up a new scarecrow the other day. I saw it from the road. Looks like a man in a big coat and wearing a hat. She has it by the old graves where her strawberries grow."

Larry thought about Finger Man and Butcher Cat. It was his best story from home. Nothing about it was real, he knew. It was a good one, though, you had to admit. Even if he had learned it in Sunday school. No, there was nothing to the story. Jessica had just wanted to keep the boys too scared to cut through the cemetery.

"Maybe you should drive by there sometime tonight, Larry, and see if she's okay. I'm afraid she'll spend all night out there, scaring off the children, tending to her scarecrow. She might just die, she stays outside this time of year."

"She's too mean to die, Momma."

That evening, Jessica put on her thickest sweater. She pulled on two pairs of socks and then her garden boots. If a body kept their feet warm, she knew, they could be warm just about anywhere. She tugged a wool cap down over her ears. The elderly woman picked up a trowel and her beanie-flipper slingshot. She had round pebbles and marbles in her coat pockets. Her arm had arthritis in it now, and she couldn't throw like she used to.

Dry autumn leaves caught in a Tuscaloosa evening breeze moved along the street as if they had somewhere to be.

Jessica wasn't giving out treats on Halloween. She'd stopped doing that years ago. The kids had soaped her windows and thrown eggs at her house. This year, any of those kids who brought eggs to her house, she'd get them with a rock, or a marble if she had to. She could see her porch from the cemetery. Jessica had a pretty clear shot when she came out from behind the new Finger Man scarecrow she'd put up.

When someone trampled the strawberry plants this time of year, it ruined them for spring. If she weren't there to keep guard, those kids would trample them for sure. She had to keep them out of the cemetery on Halloween and guard her house both. Jessica was up to the task.

That night, it was almost too dark to see. She could hear them going by on the street, those kids dressed up like ghosts. She could see them in the streetlights.

"Better not come this way," she muttered.

When the chattering voices of children came too near, Jessica stepped out from behind her scarecrow. There was a little moonlight, and she could see well enough to take aim if need be. She could see if any of the little goblins in the street came to the cemetery.

She could see that cat standing right in front of her, too. It stood on its hind legs and pawed the air. It seemed friendly enough to Jessica, friendly enough for her to keep looking.

That's when she felt the finger at her back, the bony finger that stabbed through her clothes, slipped inside her skin like a knife, and entered her spine through flesh and muscle. It was too late for stones or marbles, either one. It was too late to scream. By the time Jessica thought of it, Butcher Cat had been tossed her tongue. Fresh blood pooled inside her mouth, drooled from the corners where her lips met. Blood ran from her quivering chin.

The finger of bone held her upright while the assailant behind her made careful work of poor Jessica. He took the fingers from her left hand first, five at a time, and slipped the flesh of them over his own. Once he had the woman's eyeballs in his hat, Finger Man took the rest of her in slices. If you hear the story right the next time you're in Sunday school, he carried all of Jessica into the grave where he was buried. It is a grave in Tuscaloosa, Alabama, that is not marked with a stone. The coffin hollow is covered by strawberry vines.

Schoolchildren wandering through the cemetery sometimes hear a cat meow when they stop to pick strawberries.

Kids hear all sorts of things. Jessica's last Halloween, kids out trick-or-treating said they could hear her cackle and laugh in the cemetery when they walked by. The police found her garden boots in the graveyard, along with her two pairs of socks and the rest of her clothes. Her sweater was soaked in blood. Someone had killed her and carried off her body, the newspaper articles said. Neighbors took down the scarecrow and set it in Jessica's yard.

Larry Crawford was never sure what happened that night to Jessica Prewitt. All he knew was that no one in Tuscaloosa ever saw her again, and that the story he told his shipmates in the navy had a new way to end.

Wedding Cat

~ ~ ~ ~ ~ ~ ~ ~ ~ ~ ~ ~ ~ ~

Leave it to Faith Bailey to get married on the Appalachian Trail, Paige thought. Leave it to her college roommate to get married in North Carolina to begin with. How dare she meet and fall in love with someone from North Carolina? Paige laughed. It was easier, she supposed, than meeting the man of your life in San Diego. That certainly hadn't happened yet.

The flights from San Diego to North Carolina were a choice between two horrors. Fly all night or fly all day. She could arrive in Asheville just before midnight or at 9:00 the next morning. Paige took the night flight, leaving San Diego at 10:35. Three hours later, she was somewhere over America on a US Airways Airbus when she fell sound asleep.

At first, Paige pictured things. She saw Faith in her

bathrobe in their dorm room, wearing bunny slippers, her hair up in curlers. Before she knew it, Paige was late for her final in a class she couldn't remember having attended.

Then she was in a car, driving lazily along a road that rose and fell among lush green hills. In the dream, Paige looked out the window at the scenery. She turned onto a small road and came to a stop in front of a lovely old farmhouse with a red roof. A barn was behind the house, and steep hills rose beyond. The house was surrounded by blooming shrubs that almost reached the roof. A curving flagstone pathway led to the front porch steps. A kindly house cat was at the top of the steps, waiting. The cat was the color of blond wood.

It was a farm Paige had never seen before, but in her dream she knew she belonged there. It was waiting for her with the front door unlocked.

When she woke, the feeling of peace and comfort proved fleeting. She rethought her dream, trying to remember details, trying to recapture the feeling she had. Paige wished she knew how to find it.

Paige was thirty years old. Faith Bailey was the last of her close friends to be married. If Paige couldn't be married soon, she'd settle for that farm in her dream instead. She was tired of San Diego.

On the hop from Charlotte, the smaller plane provided a wonderful view of the North Carolina mountains as it descended to its Asheville landing. Paige yawned while signing in for her rental car. She yawned while waiting for her bags. She hoped the light teal dress would do. The bride's party was that afternoon.

She had to find her way to Hot Springs, to a place called

the Laurel Skyland Inn. Faith had given her directions. The party was supposed to be a forty-five-minute hike on the Appalachian Trail to a place called Lover's Leap. That's what the invitations said: "Bridge Street to Lover's Leap, 45 minutes. Drinks served."

Before Paige hiked anywhere, she needed to find some time to sleep. The overnight flight had exhausted her. Hot Springs was thirty-five miles north of Asheville. She ate an omelet at a Waffle House. If it had been called Omelet Hut, she probably would have ordered a waffle. *Maybe that's why I'm still single,* Paige thought.

She looked at Hot Springs on the map. It was near the Tennessee border. The area on the map was packed full of contour lines.

She was on her way first to a town named Joe. That should be easy. One road passed through there. The road to Hot Springs. Easy as pie.

By the time Paige found a town called Democrat, a town she hadn't seen on the map and wasn't looking for, she knew she was lost. She asked directions and was told to go to Jupiter, that Hot Springs was a skip and a hop from there. Paige studied the map again. Trust and Luck were on the way to Joe.

She gave up on Joe, bypassed Jupiter, and decided she needed a town named Walnut. At Walnut, she would be on the main road to Hot Springs. On the way to Walnut, she tried calling the Laurel Skyland Inn on her cell phone to ask if someone would guide her in. Paige couldn't get a signal.

The mountains were thick and green and gorgeous. There was no getting around that. Mountains rose behind the first mountains, and more mountains beyond those.

Paige found herself on a ridge road. It rolled up and down, and she went up and down right along with it. She started giggling. Then the pavement ended. *It shouldn't do that*, she thought. The ridge road turned into a descending dirt road that twisted back and forth into a deep mountain hollow. Water rushed over rocks on one side of her, falling away from the ridge as rapidly as the road.

It was a beautiful drive, even if her neck hurt and she had to go slowly because of the switchbacks. The rhododendrons along the side of the road were twenty feet tall and should be in a museum somewhere. In San Diego, rhododendrons came in five-gallon clay pots on people's back patios.

Finally, the road turned to pavement again. She drove through a low valley with sunny, rolling hills on one side that looked like pastures and orchards, the mountains rising behind. The other side of the road was a steep rise with trees that cast shade across the pavement. Paige had no idea where she was. She tried her cell phone again and still got no signal. The valley road was narrower than the others she'd been on.

Paige yawned. She thought she saw a big dog in the middle of the pavement ahead. Paige slowed down. The big dog raised its head and stared at her. It had antlers. It was a deer. Paige stopped. The stag didn't budge, his head held high and steady. The big male looked entirely over her car and beyond. Paige saw movement in her rearview mirror and spun around in her seat. Behind her, crossing from the green fields, a doe and a fawn bounded twice on the pavement and lifted, as if on wings, one behind the other, into the thick trees on the high side of the road.

When Paige turned to the front again, the stag was gone.

She could barely believe what she had seen. She wanted to tell someone.

Around the next curve was a waterfall. Water poured over rocks and splashed next to the pavement. Paige stopped with her window down to look at the cascade and listen to the rush of mountain water. A cool mist touched her cheeks. *They should put these in San Diego, too*, she thought.

She looked across the seat to where the orchards had been and saw a farmhouse instead, a lovely old farmhouse in white clapboard with a red roof. A barn lay behind the house, with rising, steep hills beyond. The house was surrounded by blooming shrubs that almost reached the roof. Paige had to see for herself. She pulled forward to a dirt-and-gravel side road, turned toward the house, and drove slowly closer.

It was the house from her dream. The house that waited for her. She couldn't see it yet, but she knew a curving flagstone pathway led to the front porch steps. And that a kindly house cat was at the top of the steps, watching. The cat would be golden blond.

A small stand of hemlocks guarded the side of the road. Paige turned the motor off and kept her window down, staring at the house, trying to remember every detail of her dream.

"Oh!" Paige said when someone tapped hard on the trunk of the rental car.

"Sorry, missy. Didn't mean to startle you."

She let out a long breath. It was an old man with a kindly face and shoulders bent forward from a life of work. He smiled under a thick shag of gray hair. All the men over thirty Paige met in San Diego were bald or on the verge.

"Hi," she said. "I'm lost."

"Looks like your car broke down to me."

"Oh, no, it's fine. I was just turning around."

The man had his hand on the side of the rental. "No," he said. "It feels more like it won't run. Might need jumper cables. I can do that for you in a jiff."

Paige didn't want to argue with the old guy. She was washed with a feeling of kindness coming from him. She was comfortable with his standing there. He seemed to belong. Instead of saying anything, she turned the key in the ignition to show him. Nothing happened. The car wouldn't start.

She smiled like a fool and opened her car door.

"I'm still lost," Paige said. "I've been driving a very long time." She stretched her back and leaned her head slowly from side to side. She felt like she should know his name.

"I can give you directions, sure thing, but won't do no good till your car starts. Tractor's in the barn. I'll bring it round. You can go on in the house, if you want to freshen up. There's sweet tea in the kitchen. You know where it is."

He nodded and walked by her, down the gravel road toward the barn, which was farther behind the farmhouse than it had looked to be from the road. Farther than it had looked in her dream.

Paige walked to the front of the farmhouse. She found the flagstone path that led to the porch steps. The red roof was metal. That surprised her. Her dream hadn't indicated what it was made of.

On the porch were two wooden rockers and a small braided rug, but no cat. Paige felt there should have been one. The front door was unlocked. She used the bathroom off the bedroom on the right and found her way to the kitchen. A pitcher of sweet tea was in the refrigerator. She found a clean glass in the cupboard. Paige wandered into the living room. She sat on the upholstered sofa for a minute and sipped iced tea.

The old man was in the leather recliner watching television with the sound turned off when she woke. Paige was under a soft quilt made of tiny circles inside bigger ones. Her stomach growled.

"What time is the wedding?" the man asked her.

Paige cleared her throat. Her glass of tea sat half full on a crocheted coaster on the coffee table. "Two o'clock. How do you know about the wedding?"

He smiled at the television. "You were telling me all about it before you fell asleep. What's her name again? Something from the Bible, is it?"

"Faith," Paige said.

A lamp on a small table beside the man's chair was turned on. A small half-mask hung from a hook in the wall. The rest of the room was dark except for the flickering light of the television. It was the dead of night.

"Your car won't start, but I can tow you into town, if we need to do it. Don't have lights that work on the tractor, though. I ran a cord out to your car and put the charger on. Don't know if it will hold, if the cells are dead in your battery. There's Kentucky Fried Chicken in the icebox, and plenty of slaw."

Paige smiled. "Thank you," she said, throwing the quilt off and sitting up. "You want some?"

"My wife had eyes like yours," the old man said, following her to the kitchen.

She found plates and put them on the table, along with utensils from the drawer. Paige pulled off two paper towels from the roll to use as napkins, one for each of them.

While they ate cold chicken and slaw, Paige found herself enjoying being there. The man might have been one of her own grandfathers, except she already knew who they were.

"What was she like?"

"She liked to have fun, my wife did. But she didn't like people to know it, so she acted stern in front of others. As soon as they were gone, she'd bust out laughing at something somebody said and would laugh all night about it. That's what I meant by saying she had eyes like yours. You have the same look in your eyes, like you're waiting till people are gone to laugh."

"How did she die?"

"Don't know that she did. Thirty-five years, and she said she wanted to be young again. I thought I'd had enough of being young myself. She just sort of disappeared."

Paige nodded, though she didn't understand.

"The cat was hers," he said.

Paige spent the night in the guest room because she had no reason not to. He had already carried her suitcases in. She could have slept in the car, but the farmhouse was safe. The old man was her friend. She could feel it in her bones. The sheets on the bed were fresh and clean. The pillows were stuffed with feathers. As she fell asleep, she could hear him snoring in another room.

When she woke, sunlight filled the room. Paige couldn't remember a single dream. She usually dreamed she was being chased at night. The chasers must have stayed in San Diego. The air smelled as if it had just rained. She stepped from the bedroom and suddenly smelled something better than rain. It smelled like hot coffee and bacon frying.

Paige came into the kitchen in time to do the eggs. She fried them hot and quick in bacon grease. The old man cut slices of raw white onion and put one on each plate.

The toast with preserves was just right. Paige ate the last bite of hers. A plastic white-and-yellow clock was on the kitchen wall above the table. Paige glanced at it, and her heart stopped.

"It's eleven o'clock!"

"I waited till the sun hit your windows to start the coffee-pot," he said. "It takes it awhile to top the hills right here along this side of the ridge. You can have the house to yourself to get ready. I'll bring that tractor back down and get your car started or hitch it up, one. Hot Springs is pretty close by."

Paige showered standing inside a plastic curtain that hung from a circle of chrome over the bathtub. The water was hot and didn't smell like chlorine. She dried her hair as best she could, letting it fall mostly to one side. She'd put her makeup on in the car. Faith wouldn't mind if Paige didn't look her best. And Paige would try not to mind that her oldest and fattest and ugliest friend, with the personality of a roll of wet toilet paper, was getting married and she herself wasn't.

She tugged on pantyhose in the bedroom and decided on the full slip under her light teal dress. Paige put on her pearls. It was a wedding, after all.

She carried her suitcases into the living room. He was sitting in the leather lounger. Light poured in through the window behind him, and his hair was illuminated by it. The television was on with the sound off.

"Set those down," he said. "I'll tote them. Your car is running fine. I jumped it six times, then checked the gas tank."

"It was empty?"

"It was." He nodded, grinning like a cat. "It's not now. I have a tank for the tractor out back."

The old man stood from his chair while Paige went back into the bedroom to get her purse.

"May I pay you for the eggs and fried chicken?"

"Now, that wouldn't be neighborly of you at all," he said. The old man rubbed his chin and glanced at the living-room wall. "But here's what you can do, if you'd like to offer my wife a favor."

Paige waited. *His wife?*

The old man pointed to the mask on the wall. "That was hers," he said. "She got it from some old boys up in the woods. It's just the top half, but she thought it was special. It's made of maple, and it's pretty old. Supposed to change anyone who wears it into a cat. Here and in Tennessee, they call it a Wampus Mask. That's the thing about her I meant to say last night. My wife loved weddings and such. Never missed one when she was young, when everybody at the church was invited."

He removed the mask from its hook. He held it in his hand as if it were alive. He smiled at the piece of wood with two holes for eyes.

"Reminds me of her," he said. "I hung it there on the wall, and it's like she's looking at me, like she's still here. I'm sentimental about it. I talk to her now and then, and we watch the TV together. I was hoping you wouldn't mind taking the mask to the wedding with you."

"So your wife may be able to see the ceremony?" Paige asked. She was touched by the love he had for his wife.

"She'd sit stern as a funeral at a wedding. Never make a peep until she got home. Then she would tell me and start laughing and laugh herself to sleep. No explaining the way that woman was. You can leave it at the desk at the inn. I'll be getting over there and will pick it up sometime soon."

"I'll be happy to," Paige said.

She reached for the wooden half-mask. It felt smooth as skin when she slipped it inside her purse.

He'd made a map for her. The drive to Bridge Street was an easy one, except for the curves and hills. Paige drove on to the Laurel Skyland Inn in time for the wedding. Rows of white folding chairs lined a short path under huge oak trees. Paige was seated on the bride's side, second row from the front. Faith Bailey's mother turned around and said hello. Paige apologized for missing the party.

A large tree branch formed a natural arch in front of the chairs. It was decorated with streamers of white flowers. Paige thought it was too pretty for words. The green lawn of the Laurel Skyland Inn was immaculate. Mountain views rose in the background.

Soon, the groom was in place, with his best man. The bridesmaids stood side by side in pink chiffon dresses with short, puffy sleeves. One was Faith's sister. They wore red shoes, and each had a wide red silk sash tied around her waist and finished in a large bow to one side. A flower girl came down the aisle, and the wedding march played. Paige tried not to stare at the groom.

Faith was too nervous to notice anyone. She took a little dip with each step as she came down the aisle in her wedding gown. Paige thought Faith might fall over when she dipped.

Faith's father seemed to think so, too. He held her by the arm. Each time she did her dipping step, it looked as if Faith were trying to pull away from him and fall over.

Once the ceremony was under way, Paige's purse fell in the grass against her ankle. She picked it up and set it on her legs, remembering the mask just in time.

"Do you, Patricia Faith Bailey, take this man . . ."

Paige opened her purse to lift out the mask. It was a sentimental gesture and a small favor for the old man and his missing wife. But instead of seeing the mask when she glanced down, Paige saw two green eyes staring back at her. A cat was in her purse. The eyes were alive. She could barely believe it. A cat was in her purse, but not for long.

". . . in sickness and in health, to love . . ."

The cat was the color of the maple-wood mask, with a short, smooth coat that glistened over its sleek muscles. It climbed out of her purse and planted its hind paws on Paige's knees, its front paws stretching to the back of the chair in front of her.

". . . and to cherish, till death do you part?"

Paige was afraid to move. The perfectly blond cat pointed its pink nose at the bride and stared intently at the proceedings.

When Patricia Faith Bailey opened her mouth to say "I do," she meowed instead.

Paige giggled. Everyone had heard it.

The bride's eyes widened noticeably. Her mouth trembled. She tried again.

"Meow, meow," Faith said loudly, clearly.

The cat wagged its tail.

The officiating minister placed his hand on the bride's shoulder.

Faith tried one more time. "Meow," she said slowly. Her eyes crossed as she stared at her own nose, try to see her mouth. She dropped her bouquet. "Me-ooow!"

Everyone from the first row back laughed. Faith's mother leapt to her feet, spilling her chair. The cat leapt with her, finding momentary purchase on her shoulder.

Paige quickly checked her purse. She couldn't find the mask. It wasn't there.

The cat turned in a circle on Faith's mother's shoulder and stretched its head high to see over the crowd. Its eyes looked like big green marbles. Paige swore she saw the cat smile. It looked right at Paige and slowly closed one eye, then let it open. The cat winked at her. Paige grinned, knowing she'd been had.

"Me-ooow!" Faith screamed, swatting at her own mouth. The cat had her tongue.

She'd meow until the cat was wood again.

Paige hoped the old man would enjoy his wife's telling him about this one. She hoped he would like hearing how the bridesmaids looked like pink pigs done up for Christmas. She hoped he would have as much fun as if he'd actually seen it.

Whoever carved that mask knew what he was doing.

Mostly There Cat

≈ ≈ ≈ ≈ ≈ ≈ ≈ ≈ ≈ ≈ ≈ ≈ ≈ ≈ ≈

High tide came with the dark moon. It was always thus.

And with the rising tide the ocean brought to shore bits and pieces of the sea, things lost. Shells and bones. After strong storms, treasure hunters combed the beaches for items washed ashore from shipwrecks. On a very lucky day, a beachcomber might find a porcelain saucer, an antique bottle or two, or perhaps a silver coin resting in the sand and seaweed. Small pieces from shipwrecks take their time—in some cases, hundreds of years—coming ashore.

The cat of George Burrows Thomas, a Welsh seaman originally from Ystrad Flur, valley to the Wye, late quartermaster of the sloop *Delight*, Francis Spriggs captain, searched the sands near Myrtle Beach each morning after the tide was out. The cat, Stripe, came on the sole mission to find bones in the sand. Those who saw the cat thought it was mostly there. This was because parts of the cat were missing.

Kimberly was sixteen when her mother took her to an off-season rental near the coastal sands along Huntington Beach State Park, south of the Myrtle Beach airport. It was time, she was informed, for a mother-daughter vacation. She was told they needed to get to know each other better.

"I can't believe it," Kimberly said on the drive. "You shouldn't make me miss a month of school just to get to know me better."

"I need to get away for a while."

"Bull," Kimberly said.

"I'm going to write my novel. It's time. And you're between boyfriends. Next thing I know, you'll be head over heels in love, and I'll never see you again."

"Bull, bull, bull. You're leaving Dad."

Her mother made a face. "It's not as simple as that, young lady. It's just a short separation. And you know I've always dreamed of living by the ocean."

The rental was a tiny neglected bungalow with two small bedrooms and one bathroom. At least Kimberly had her own room, even if it wasn't much bigger than a walk-in closet with a window. The sea made noise all the time. It was distracting.

The bungalow had no television. Kimberly had nothing to do. And nothing to wear she wanted anyone to see her wearing.

Her mother had bought her three pairs of creased cotton shorts with pockets for the beach. The shorts had half-inch cuffs.

"Who would wear those?" Kimberly wanted to know.

The pairs were bright yellow, bright pink, and bright green. Her mother had bought her three matching tops, white cotton blouses you could almost see through, with square-cut bottoms that reached below her hips. The sleeveless blouses had flat, open collars and buttoned down the front. The button rows were decorated with machine-embroidered flowers in yellow, in pink, and in green. Matching embroidered flowers were on the collars.

"Where did you find these?" Kimberly asked.

"You wear them unbuttoned, dear, over your swimsuit."

Kimberly didn't think so. She didn't own a bathing suit she could wear in front of her mom. And she wasn't going swimming in the first place.

Her mother needed time alone, she said. She sat in the house with a yellow legal pad in her lap and a felt-tip pen in her hand. Their first morning in the rental, her mother wrote "Chapter One" in bold block letters at the top of the page. She waited. She tapped the pen against her knee. Then she jumped up, told Kimberly she was going to get donuts, and drove off in the car.

Kimberly put on the green shorts, a T-shirt, and sneakers. She kicked around outdoors. The birds made too much noise. The ocean kept looking like it was coming to get her. Kimberly was afraid of the ocean. It was too big. Too big to get along with. It was full of leeches, sea snakes, biting turtles, sharks, and yucky jellyfish. Lobsters and crabs. Nothing you ever wanted to touch. The ocean, she believed, was full of fish poop and seaweed.

The beach was awful, too. It smelled bad. She walked here

and there aimlessly, trying to avoid the ocean.

The beach held nothing at all of interest to her until she saw the cat. Kimberly was walking in the tall grass behind a low sand dune when she saw something with stripes digging in the sand. It was a cat with three legs and a rear wooden one strapped to its hip. She had never seen a cat with an artificial limb before.

"Someone has made a wooden leg for a cat," she told her mother. "And it didn't seem to have a tail."

"That's nice," her mother said. "Put more zinc oxide on your nose when you go back out."

"It was talking, Mother. Talking and digging. It said something about bones."

"I see."

"At first, I thought it didn't have a tail, but here's the thing. It carried its tail around in its mouth. It laid the tail down when it wanted to dig. And it wasn't the cat that was talking. It was the cat's parrot. Well, actually, it was just a parrot head. A white parrot, you know that kind? With yellow feathers on the top of its head. It rode around on the back of the cat by clamping a piece of fur in its beak. When it wanted to talk, it let go, fell off, and then started talking."

Kimberly's mother stared hard at her daughter.

"And what did the parrot say, darling?"

" '*Aaawk*.' " Kimberly mimicked the parrot head. " 'Find a bone. *Aaawk*, no bone. Find a bone. *Aaawk*.' "

"Ready for lunch, then?"

The next morning, Kimberly found the cat on the beach again. It was farther from the bungalow. The cat had dug several holes by the time she showed up. It dug another one as she watched. It propped its rear end on its good hind leg and the wooden one, then furiously scooped sand with its front paws, piling it up behind. The cat was a gray-and-black tabby. Its tail rested nearby on the sand.

Kimberly came a few steps closer. As she neared, a white-and-yellow-feathered head rose from the hole. It had huge black eyes, one of which looked right at her. The cat was backing up out of the hole in the sand. The bird head came with it.

The cat's wooden leg was fixed to its rear hip with leather straps. When the cat was out of the sand entirely, she could see it wore a collar. A gold disk dangled from the collar.

The cat watched Kimberly, and Kimberly watched the cat.

The parrot started to talk, letting go of the cat. "*Aaawk*," it said, falling to the sand.

It pulled itself along in the sand with its beak. It paused next to the cat, then pulled itself aboard by clamping its beak on a piece of cat fur. The cat picked up its tail in its mouth and cantered away at a brisk pace. Kimberly stared in wonder as the odd duo disappeared into the tall grass at the edge of the beach.

Kimberly ran back to the bungalow. She searched through everything and finally found a rusty trowel and a small shovel in the little shed attached to the back. She eagerly returned to the holes the mostly there cat had dug in the sand. Kimberly dug each hole bigger.

"'*Aaawk*,'" she whispered to herself. "'Find a bone!'"

She returned to each enlarged hole and dug it even wider. Eventually, Kimberly found a little sea-washed bone of some sort. The size of the middle of one of her fingers, it was worn smooth and was dark brown in color.

Kimberly was exhausted and a little sunburned at the end of the day. She put the bone on the dresser in her room. She was going to show it to her mom, but her mom wouldn't believe her anyway.

Kimberly was almost asleep when she heard a scratching sound at her window screen. She was startled by the noise. Someone was trying to break in. Before she could yell for her mother, Kimberly heard a familiar squawk.

"Aye, matey! *Aaawk!*"

The parrot head was fastened by the tip of its beak to her window screen. It left its beak open and stuck out its tongue to talk. The long yellow feathers on the back of its head moved up and down as it peered into Kimberly's room with its big black eyes.

"It's you," Kimberly said in a normal voice.

"Gold for bones," the parrot said. "*Aaawk!*"

"I have one," the sixteen-year-old announced excitedly. "Right there."

"Gold for bones," the bird said again.

Its beak slipped out of the screen, and the bird head dropped from view.

"Bird overboard, *aaawk, aaawk!*" it screeched as it fell.

Kimberly rushed to the window. It was dark outside. There was very little moonlight. She could still see the cat in the yard, its tail in its mouth. The cat was mostly shadow. It walked to the white parrot head to help it climb up.

"Gold for bones," the bird said again, then grabbed a piece

of cat fur and flipped itself onto the cat's back, where it found a better hold for the ride home.

Kimberly went to sleep wondering where the cat lived.

Early the next morning, she returned to the holes in the sand. They had been filled in by the tide. The cat's tracks were washed away. Kimberly scoured the higher dunes for any sign of the cat's hasty departure the day before. Gnats and sweat bees circled her. She found trails through the grass and, through the prickly short weeds with little purple flowers, narrow footpaths she hadn't noticed earlier. She followed each one, winding this way and coming back, until she found the cat's tracks, three paws and a peg, then three paws and a peg again.

Kimberly hurried after them. Far away from the water, the earth was more tightly packed. She hoped she was on the right trail. Once in a while, she found a little round hole that might have been made by the cat's peg leg, but any paw prints were gone by then.

Then she realized she was lost. A pile of old building stones was far in front of her. Kimberly turned a complete circle, looking at everything. The sun was there. She could hear the ocean. She could find her way back.

She walked slowly onward. About ready to abandon the hunt, she heard a parrot squawk. No words, just a squawk.

Then she heard another one. The sounds were coming from the pile of rocks. Kimberly climbed on the stones and listened. She bent over to hear better.

"Oh!" She gasped when she looked up and saw the striped cat on the rocks, its tail in its mouth. "I have it here," she said.

Kimberly removed the bone from her pocket and held it out in her hand toward the cat. The cat put down its tail. It watched Kimberly with its head held low, ears back. It looked as if it were about to leap at her.

She stepped away from the cat, almost tumbling off the rocks. More carefully, she backed away a little farther. The cat let its tail drop and picked up the small brown bone. It hurried away over the stones. Kimberly stared at the cat's striped tail. It wasn't a minute before the cat was back to pick it up. Then it was gone again over the rocks.

An echoing version of the parrot's phrase lifted from inside the pile of rocks.

"Gold for bones!" the voice said. It was a deep voice, not a squawk or a screech. It was a man's voice.

She must have been standing on a grave, Kimberly figured.

"Aye, the lass," the man's voice boomed from underground again. "Give to her the gold she earned this day."

Kimberly ran away. She didn't know what to tell her mom, so she didn't say anything.

The next morning, Kimberly showered, ate breakfast, and stayed in the house. She borrowed one of her mother's books. She read sitting at the little dinette table in the kitchen, pushing six stacked boxes of donuts out of her way. She read sitting on the couch.

"Why don't you go somewhere, dear?" her mother asked. "People are on the beach today, and the breeze feels marvelous."

Kimberly didn't know how to tell her mother that she was afraid of ghosts. She went into her room and read, sitting on the bed. She read only a page or two, then thought through everything she had seen and heard. She put the book down and rolled onto her side to look out the window. Something shiny glinted on the window sill.

She brought her face to the screen and stared at the object. The cat and the parrot had come back. Kimberly had slept through their visit. She dashed outside to bring in the shiny object.

It was a gold coin, bright as new. A raised cross was in the middle of the coin, with castle towers and cats in the spaces between the equal arms of the cross. The cats were standing and pawing the air. Maybe they were lions, she decided. On the other side were two skinny towers or trees with the numeral 8 at the top, and the letters L, P, and V. Words were printed around the outside edges of the coin on both sides, but the tops of the letters weren't there. The gold coin was about an inch and quarter across. It was heavy for its size. She bet it was worth a lot.

Ghost or not, Kimberly wasn't afraid any longer. Not in the daylight. She returned to the rocks with her shovel and searched the formation with more care. Around the far side, she found a stone-cluttered entrance to a cellar. She could have found it yesterday if she had looked. If she hadn't been scared off.

The stones were the ruins of an old lighthouse foundation. She heard voices inside. She had to move only two heavy rocks with her shovel. Old stone steps led down to a doorway. Kimberly climbed down and put her hands on the old wooden frame. The door was gone. A flicker of light came from inside the hole.

Kimberly wiped her hands on her shorts, retrieved her shovel, and stepped inside. She hoped she didn't have smudges of dirt on her face.

The cat was there, curled on the top of an old wooden table. Its tail was nearby. A candle burned on a small tray on the table. The gray-and-black tail wagged twice on its own. Apparently, the cat didn't mind company.

"*Aaawk!*" the parrot head screeched. "Ahoy!"

Kimberly turned to see that the bird head was not alone. It rested among parts of a bearded sea captain stacked in the corner. The bird head may have been perched on the captain's shoulder, if all of the parrot and all of the man had been there.

The bearded head of George Burrows Thomas, a Welsh seaman originally from Ystrad Flur, valley to the Wye, late quartermaster of the sloop *Delight*, Francis Spriggs captain, sat among a clutter of sea clothes and body parts. Almost one whole leg was there, but it wasn't connected to anything. Both eyes in the sailor's head were a brilliant blue.

"Grateful to you, lass, and to the Lord Almighty," the head said. "Ring finger, it was. Very grateful indeed."

"You're welcome, sir," Kimberly said, quite uncertain how one should properly address a talking head.

"That be Stripe the cat," he said, rolling his blue eyes toward the table. "And you have had the pleasure of saying hello to my talking bird, I believe. From Honduras, 'tis. I never come to naming it."

"*Aaawk!*" the parrot head began. "Find a—"

The sea captain's head told it to shut up. A hand lifted from the cellar floor. The cat leapt from the table, leaving its tail, to sit by the hand, which soon caressed its furry back.

"I'm Kimberly." She tried to smile.

"Aye, Lady Kimberly it is. And a strapping lass you be. Now, tell me quick, for I am an old, old man of the sea. Will you find more bones for me?"

Kimberly nodded.

"I be George Burrows Thomas, of Ystrad Flur, valley to the Wye in Wales, before I took to the sea for my maturity, then quartermaster of the sloop *Delight*, of equal rank to Captain Francis Spriggs, except in time of battle, aye."

The head had a story to tell. Kimberly found a comfortable stone to lean against.

"The *Delight* was a fine and speedy craft," he said, "with a crew of three score and fifteen. Fast in shallows and fast at sea."

The sloop *Delight* was taken by a hurricane. All twelve cannons were dropped in a desperate attempt to keep her afloat in the horrible storm. The quartermaster rescued the ship's treasury, his cat, Stripe, and the parrot from Honduras by drifting from the sinking mast in a small wooden rowboat. The tiny wooden craft was caught by a massive wave and carried in one large sweep a half-mile closer to the South Carolina coast before going under.

"Were any saved?" Kimberly asked.

"Not to worry, lass. She flew the skeleton and hourglass on black for our flag. Pirates one and all, well prepared for the watery grave. Their bones didn't catch the tide, you see. Serves them well and good to stay as far away as your pretty little head dares to dream. Nary a one who did not deserve to be in chains."

Before leaving, Kimberly asked if the odd trio needed food.

"Nay," the head of George Burrows Thomas replied. "We're dead."

Kimberly nodded slowly, trying to understand.

"We're dead, but this isn't a proper grave as yet for the likes of we. Not until we're complete, you see? I wasn't buried at sea. I died there, but I wasn't buried, except to drift across the wretched bottom, piece by piece like the pieces of a broken ship. I died there, but I'll be buried here, as soon as I get the rest of me."

"I have two more weeks to look," Kimberly told him, promising to work diligently.

"No rush atall," the head said. "But when you're good and through, you might leave the shovel here with me in the rocks. Come in handy later, that would."

The cat meowed. It was the first time it had made a sound in front of Kimberly.

Stripe was probably tired of digging, Kimberly decided. She figured it all out once she had time to think about it thoroughly. The cat had swum closer to shore than the other two during the hurricane. She imagined a big fish had eaten the parrot except for the head. And George? He probably sank right away, along with the ship's treasury.

When Kimberly's mother packed the car at the end of their stay, Kimberly had nine gold 1715 Lima escudos in her suitcase, each one as fresh as the year it was coined. She told her mother she wanted to come back to the crummy beach and the tiny bungalow as soon as they could.

"You'll be driving next year," her mother said. "You can come back anytime you like, as long as you clear it with me and your father first."

"Aye," Kimberly agreed. "Fair winds and Godspeed."

Piano Cat
~ ~ ~ ~ ~ ~ ~ ~ ~ ~ ~ ~ ~ ~ ~

That Wednesday morning in November, Arnold Endicott opened the tabletop Victrola on the dresser, cranked the handle a few rounds, and carefully lowered the needle into place. The thick one-sided recording of "Shine On, Harvest Moon" was the only record he owned.

Arnold waited for company. The recording was a duet.

He was a permanent resident in an assisted living facility. It used to be a nursing home. He kept the volume low and hummed along. Most people would have heard the warp and the scratches in the old record. Arnold, though, experienced the music as brand new. It was sweet to hear, so sweet and clear. He heard it that way every time, as if he were listening to the classic romantic duet with his young wife, Beatrice, so many years ago. His arm was around her still. He could smell perfume in her hair.

The orange-striped cat was quick to the window of Arnold's room. The scratchy song on the old Victrola was his call to breakfast. The cat was a companionable stray that had visited Arnold's window one night and then come inside when Arnold pushed his fist through a lower corner of the window screen. They'd been friends ever since. The orange-striped cat liked Arnold. And the old man liked breaking the rules.

It's either have a cat or buy a gun and rob a bank, Arnold thought.

He named the cat Clyde. The cat enjoyed the world outside. Arnold was just fine with that. Arnold Endicott had lived there once himself, and the world came highly recommended.

Arnold combed his hair carefully. It was just a few white wisps these days. Clyde groomed himself on Arnold's bed. The duo had their routine. Clyde started with his ears and moved to the back of his head. Arnold combed his hair from the side.

The old man dressed in his best shirt and bowtie. It was perhaps too cool for his seersucker suit, but it was his only suit now. Besides, a walk outdoors would keep him warm. Arnold put on his wingtip dress shoes from the closet. Clyde watched him tie the strings. Arthritis made it difficult.

"Keep an eye on things," Arnold said. He lifted the needle from his only record, pushed the window screen loose entirely, and climbed outside, nearly landing on his face. It was one of Arnold's annual escapes. Clyde watched him leave.

Grocery stores were so much better than they used to be. You could eat lunch there now. They had whole buffets, and little tables set up with chairs. They were regular restaurants.

Arnold paid for a cold bottle of Hires cream soda at the check-out counter. His hands shook. He gave the clerk two dollars and told her to keep the change. She opened the soda pop for him. A few bubbles of cream soda ran down his chin when he took a drink. *Just like a little kid*, he thought. So what if he dribbled pop on his chin? It was either that or rob the place.

The store was crowded the day before Thanksgiving. Arnold knew it would be. He was there looking for someone. He shuffled up and down the aisles, trying not to spill his pop when a cart came his way. One of his wingtips came untied. He didn't notice.

Arnold said hello to everyone. Some people said hello back. Those were the ones who captured his closer attention.

He ended up at a large display of whole turkeys in the meat department. A young woman pushed a cart with three kids in tow. She was only sixty or so. He guessed the kids were her grandchildren. She called one of them Willa Dean. Arnold liked the name.

She wore thick glasses. Her curly hair was gray and cut close to her head. Her shoes were as badly worn as her large leather purse. Arnold thought she might be the one he was looking for. She picked up a turkey. Arnold looked at the other items in her cart. One of the kids ran off, and she hollered him back.

"Looks like a fine dinner you're making there," Arnold said.

"I'm doing my best, if I don't forget the pumpkin pie." She smiled at Arnold. Mavis knew his kind. He was one of the lonely seniors who showed up at the holidays just to be around people. You saw them in all the stores.

"I'm sure you won't." Arnold smiled back. He hoped his teeth stayed in place.

He lagged behind but continued to watch the woman. She took her wallet out of her purse and seemed to be counting her money. She was the one, he decided. Flour and butter and eggs were in her cart. Not one frozen piecrust. Four packages of dinner rolls, though. Two loaves of bread, two gallons of milk, two large cans of pumpkin, and a carton of whipping cream, among the other things.

Arnold made his way to the front of the store. He stood patiently before a tall stack of factory-made fireplace logs. He'd set down his pop and didn't remember where.

When the lady with the three grandkids came to the counter, Arnold shuffled that way. He stood at the end of the counter as if he belonged there and fiddled with her bags when they were placed in her cart. She thought he was trying to look as if he were helping out. Sometimes, old folks pretended they were working at a place. Or maybe this one had worked in a grocery store once and was confused whether or not he still did.

When the clerk announced the total, Mavis opened her wallet.

Arnold was ahead of the game. He leaned forward and handed the clerk the money he held in his hand.

"Thank you, Mr. Endicott," the clerk said.

Arnold had already turned away. The clerk had heard he came into the stores, particularly this one, once in a while.

Mavis stared after Arnold, her mouth wide open, then told the grandkids to hush. She was soon distracted when the clerk handed her the receipt and more than eighty dollars in change.

"Lord Almighty," Mavis said. "What in heaven's name is that?"

"Mr. Endicott wants you to have a happy Thanksgiving, ma'am," the clerk told her.

"No, he can't do that. I don't even know the man."

In the end, Arnold Endicott could do pretty much what he wanted, Mavis learned. That lonely old man owned the entire chain of A & B Food Stores across the South. His first one was in Atlanta. The store she shopped in was built where the first one had been. It was just Arnold's Fruits and Vegetables back then, before he married Beatrice.

Mavis accepted the money from the clerk. She looked around the parking lot for the old man. She was going to make that codger take back his change. But he wasn't there. Arnold had gone to the men's room at the back of the deli. He took his time. Mavis gave up and got the grandkids into the car.

While she unpacked the groceries in her kitchen, one of the grandchildren tinkered with the upright piano, playing one key at a time. They were not allowed to do that. Soon, they'd all be banging on the keys. Mavis walked into the living room with her hands on her hips, ready to pull someone off the piano bench.

No one was there. The three kids sat on the couch in a row, watching television.

"Who played that piano? Willa Dean?"

All three children shook their heads. It was usually Willa Dean who played the piano, but she never lied about it when she did.

"Grandma has to cook," Mavis told them. "You-all be good now, and I'll bake cinnamon and sugar curls." Mavis regularly used the leftover pie dough to make treats for the grandchildren when they stayed at her house, which was often as not with these three.

When she put the first gallon of milk in the refrigerator, Mavis saw a green piece of paper stuck to one side. It was a hundred-dollar bill.

"Lord Almighty," she said.

She went through the grocery bags and found seven more. That old coot had given her a thousand dollars, food included.

That night, Mavis heard the piano playing again. It was faint and light. One key at a time. It sounded to Mavis like a song she knew, but she couldn't place it. She was going to head downstairs and see who was up, but she fell asleep instead.

Thanksgiving dinner was a large family affair at Mavis's house. While everyone was eating, the lady in the thick glasses told her story one more time.

"I have his name," she said. "I looked it up in the phone book. As soon as we're done, while you girls wash the dishes, I'm carrying a plate of food to his house. And a pie. Don't anyone touch that last pie. That belongs to Mr. Arnold Endicott."

She heard the piano again. Mavis looked around the two tables set up in the dining room and counted faces. Everyone was there. It was the same song. She'd been hearing it off and on since breakfast. One key at a time. Despite herself, she scooted back from the table and walked into the living room. The piano bench was empty. The lid on the spinet piano was up. She had closed it when she walked by that morning.

The song sounded like a memory. No one at the table said a thing about it. Mavis feared she was the only one who heard it. She feared she was losing her hearing.

"I've been hearing that piano all morning," she told her family. "What is that song? It sounds familiar. I must be losing my mind."

Mavis left family scattered about the house. She drove to Mr. Endicott's house. It was a nice neighborhood, and she expected as much. That old man might be rich as the devil, but he was lonely as sin. She came alone to spend some time with him without having the kids distract her. Old people liked to talk whenever somebody would listen.

She drove up the circular driveway and parked. Mavis left the pumpkin pie on the seat. She carried the covered plate of turkey and dressing, mashed potatoes and gravy, corn and green beans to the front porch. Tall white columns decorated the steps to the house.

Two slat-back porch chairs were in front of the doors, a piece of yellow rope tied between them. A cardboard No Trespassing sign was stapled to the nylon rope. Arnold Endicott was lonelier than she'd realized. Between the long brass handles of the twin front doors were a chain and padlock. Mavis set the Thanksgiving dinner on one of the tied-up chairs.

He must be coming and going from around back, she thought. She walked to the side of the house. A man was standing there smoking a cigarette. He was embarrassed to see Mavis. He smiled awkwardly and held the cigarette out in front of him, as if to explain.

"I'm at Mom's house for Thanksgiving," he said. He nodded to the house next door. "I was going to take the cigarette butt with me when I was through."

"I'm sure you were," Mavis said. "I have something for Mr. Endicott around front. Do you know where I should leave it for him? I was hoping he could have it today."

"Oh, he doesn't live here anymore. He moved into the nursing home a few years ago. Dad keeps the yard up for him and makes sure the heat comes on, so the pipes don't freeze. I heard today that they'll be selling the house pretty soon. My dad has the key, if you need to get inside."

The nursing home was called Willows Assisted Living. *Willows in Atlanta*, Mavis thought. *I guess there might be a few.*

Mavis knew how to get there. She walked back to the porch to pick up the Thanksgiving dinner for Mr. Endicott. An orange cat was nosing the covered meal as Mavis approached.

"Scat!" She waved her hand, and the cat was gone.

Mavis carried the meal into the reception area of the nursing home. She'd bring the pie in after she talked to Mr. Endicott.

A nurse came from the hallway when Mavis asked the receptionist if she could speak to Mr. Arnold Endicott.

"Everyone loved Arnold," the nurse said. "Such a gentleman. And he fed that cat. We all knew." She smiled. "We'll replace the screen now that he's gone, bless his soul. Don't know what we'll do with the cat."

"Gone?"

"Why, yes, dear. Arnold Endicott passed away Tuesday night. You didn't know?"

"No." Mavis meant, *No, he didn't.* The nurse had her days wrong. It couldn't have been Tuesday.

"In his sleep," the nurse said. "It was sad, his having to go like that just before Thanksgiving. It was his favorite holiday. Funny that, Arnold having no family and all. He'd go to the supermarket every year and buy someone's groceries for them. Did it since he moved here. It was his grocery store, after all. Probably did it his whole life."

"Excuse me," the receptionist interrupted. "Are you Mrs. Mundee, by any chance?"

"Yes, Mavis Mundee," she said.

"I'm so glad I asked." The receptionist put her hand to her chest. "Mr. Endicott left something for you. It's in his room." She stood from behind her desk and smiled at Mavis. "Follow me," she said.

Mavis looked at the wooden box on the dresser. It had a domed lid and a crank handle on one side. She knew what it was. Mavis wasn't born yesterday. A yellow post-it note on the lid had *Mavis Mundee* written in ballpoint pen by a shaking hand.

She set the covered plate of Thanksgiving food on the dresser next to the Victrola. She opened the lid.

"Go ahead," the receptionist said.

Mavis cranked the handle and watched the record spin. She raised the chrome arm that held the needle and lowered it onto the record. She stepped back with a hand on her hip to listen. The recording sounded scratchy, and the volume increased and decreased according to the warp in the record. It was a duet, "Shine On, Harvest Moon." Mavis recognized the song instantly. It was the one that had been playing on her piano since she arrived home from the grocery store yesterday morning.

The orange-striped cat came in through the window. He jumped to Mr. Endicott's bed and walked back and forth on the covers, meowing loudly for food.

The receptionist laughed. "That's Mr. Endicott's cat," she said. "His name is Clyde. He's trying to sing. Mr. Endicott taught him that."

Mavis slipped a small piece of turkey from Mr. Endicott's Thanksgiving plate and held it out to the cat while the record played. Clyde stopped stalking, walked to her hand, and thrust his whiskers out. He smelled the baked meat, tasting it as cats do, by its scent.

"Clyde's just an old stray," the receptionist told her. "He lives under the window. Mr. Endicott snuck food from the cafeteria to feed the cat for quite some time. He loved that cat. We all pretended not to know, so no one would get into trouble. The center has a no-pet rule."

The orange-striped cat took the turkey from Mavis. He carried it to another part of the bed and set it down. Clyde chewed a small piece of the tasty treat with his tail up in the air.

"I don't know what we're going to do with that cat," the receptionist said. "I guess we'll have to call Animal Control. That would be better for Clyde than living outdoors in the city. Dogs might catch up with him, you know."

"I do know," Mavis told her. "And I know what we're going to do."

It would serve the grandchildren right if they got scratched once every little while when they were too rambunctious in the house.

"If you will carry the record player for me, I'll carry the cat," Mavis said.

Once Mavis was back in the car, the receptionist carried the pumpkin pie into the nursing home. "You can pass it around if you want to, dear," Mavis had told her. "Or take it home for yourself, you've been such a help to me and Mr. Endicott."

On the way home, with the Victrola in the backseat and the orange cat sitting next to it, Mavis hummed "Shine On, Harvest Moon." Clyde meowed.

"Hush, now," Mavis said. "Guess I raised more cats than children in my day. You be quiet and behave." Eight hundred dollars and change would buy a lot of cat food, she figured. "And don't you go running off like you did at his house, you hear? Lord Almighty, you'll be in trouble but good, you try those cat shenanigans on me."

The dishes were done when Mavis came home. Some of the family members were gone. The others had a football game going on TV. Two of the grandchildren were spending the night. The cat kept mostly in the kitchen, where his food and water dishes were. He stayed away from everyone, watching the movements inside the house from under the kitchen table.

Late that night, when everyone was in bed, Mavis heard the piano. One key at a time, like a cat walking. Not too loud. It was "Shine On, Harvest Moon," but you could barely recognize it. Mavis didn't know who was playing it, the cat or Mr. Endicott. It was something nice to listen to, she decided.

As she fell asleep, she remembered her husband and the way he liked to dance.

No-Smoking Cat

"I felt the cat on my lips this morning," Alyssa told her coworkers at the zydeco bar. The bar was between Jackson and Lee streets. Alyssa worked nights.

"Sure," Muse Hawkins said. "All the ghosts came up this way from Katrina. Cat ghosts especially. They left the coast days before the hurricane hit. Cats know when bad weather is coming."

"I don't think it's from the hurricane," she said when Muse came back from the kitchen with a tray of washed glasses for the bar. "I think it's the cat that died when my uncle did, when he burned the top floor off the house."

"Cat might want to stay where it always lived."

"It was there when I moved in with my aunt. I'm sure of it, Muse. It doesn't bother me any. Just sometimes at night, I can feel its whiskers cross my lips. It wakes me up, is all. I feel it on my lips."

"You ever seen it yet?"

"No. My aunt doesn't see it either, so I guess it's not really there."

The door-to-door missionaries had seen it, though. Alyssa was certain of that. They had looked down in their twin hair-cuts and seen the ghost.

They stood together in white shirts and black ties, one of them talking to Alyssa at the front door. The other stared past her at a low place in front of the basement door. His eyes went big, and his face froze. All of a sudden, he turned white as ice.

He nudged his partner hard and pointed. Then the one who was talking saw it. His eyes got big, too. And he stopped talking. You can't get a missionary to stop talking once you open the door, but that cat did.

Alyssa turned around to look behind her. Nothing was there to see. When she turned back to the door, the missionaries were running down the walk to the street. They didn't say goodbye or leave her a single piece of literature.

She liked the cat that wasn't there, except for the whiskers across her lips at night. Maybe she could learn to live with it, now that she knew she wasn't feeling spiders on her lips. The dead kitty meant no harm, she figured.

"Wouldn't bother me any. I don't go to bed till morning anyway," Muse said.

He strapped on his accordion and walked into the corner where the band played. Alyssa picked up her tray of drinks and gumbo and looked around the bar for the people who'd ordered them.

The missionaries weren't the only ones. Alyssa's boyfriend had seen it, too. Alyssa didn't know that. But even if she had, she wouldn't have told Muse a thing about it. Her boyfriend was a secret from her aunt. He was a secret from everyone else, for that matter. Gil was a married man. He wouldn't be for much longer. But until then, Alyssa was discreet. She never mentioned his name.

Gil had yelped awake in the early morning because he said someone had thrown a glass of water on him. He thought it was Alyssa.

She'd been dead asleep with the angels, she told him.

His face was wet, and so was his pillow. He said it wasn't the least bit funny. A glass was on the nightstand right next to him.

"You tried to drink it in your sleep," Alyssa told him. "Then you woke up."

"I didn't throw a glass of water on my own head."

"Well, I didn't either. So there."

Gil tossed the wet pillow on the floor. He lay back on the bed with his hands on his chest. He hadn't told Alyssa the truth. Gil hadn't been asleep. He had waited for her to fall off, and then he'd lit a cigarette. He was going to use the glass of water as an ashtray. Then someone threw it in his face. The more he thought, the more it seemed like he must have done it himself.

The reason he didn't tell Alyssa was that her aunt maintained a strict no-smoking rule for the house. Since the night her husband had fallen asleep smoking and burned the top floor, no smoking of any kind was allowed in the house. Gil had to sneak up the basement stairs and walk outside to smoke. It was too much trouble to get dressed and go outside to have a cigarette.

Gil stared up at the darkness for two minutes with no pillow under his head, then got up and left. He wasn't supposed to be there anyway.

The night after Alyssa told Muse about the cat on her face, Gil came by the bar for last call. The band was through. The tables were mostly empty. He sat at the bar, showing off to the other waitress. Gil flipped a lit cigarette inside his mouth, held it there with his mouth closed, then flipped it back out again, still burning.

"It looks like you're kissing yourself," the younger waitress said. "It looks like you're a monkey in the zoo."

"Well, now, darling, I'd rather be kissing you." Gil was drunk.

He combed his hair like Jerry Lee Lewis. Alyssa could tell from across the room when Gil was drunk. He pushed his hand over his hair, forgot what he was doing, and left it there.

Alyssa drove Gil home in her car. He was spending the night, it looked like. He smoked in the car, leaning back in the passenger seat with his eyes closed. Alyssa reached across and rolled his window down to let the smoke out.

"That's your last one tonight," she said.

Stumbling, he followed Alyssa to the door of her aunt's house. He was singing a song that had been on the radio.

"And try to be quiet for once, will you? My aunt catches you one time, that will be the last you ever come here. She'll make sure of that. You're as drunk as a skunk. Now, hush."

When Alyssa got out of bed to visit the bathroom upstairs, Gil rolled onto his side, away from the light. She had turned on the nightstand lamp on her side. She slipped into her chenille robe and left the door open a crack.

His stomach rumbled. Gil was awake just enough to want a cigarette. The lights came on in the hallway. Gil reached around on the floor looking for his clothes, to find his shirt pocket with the half-pack of cigarettes.

Gil was dying for a smoke. He'd use his shoe for an ashtray if he had to. He waited until he heard the stairs creak under Alyssa's feet, then lit one up.

As soon as his cigarette was lit, the light bulb in Alyssa's bedside lamp burned out with a tiny snapping sound. The room was dark except for the slice of light spilling through the crack in the door.

The light in the doorway grew bigger as the door swung slowly open. A tall, dark shadow stood in the door. The shadow wore a funny-looking hat. Gil stared, squinting. It looked like Alyssa with a bunch of hair piled on top of her head. But it was too tall to be Alyssa or her aunt, and too dark. Even in the light of the hallway, the figure looked like charcoal.

Gil saw a pair of golden eyes on top of the head. They moved. They seemed to have their own source of light. They moved again. The only thing Gil could figure out was that the figure's hat had eyes. Then he saw its tail move. Gil was mortified.

The charcoal man had a cat on his head.

The air in the room smelled like dead fish. The charcoal man walked slowly to the foot of Alyssa's bed. The door was fully open. Light poured in the room from the hallway, but Gil still couldn't clearly see the man. Then Gil realized that the man was burnt, and so was the cat. They looked like shadows even in the light. Except for the cat's yellow eyes, everything was the color of ashes.

The figure leaned forward from the foot of the bed and slowly raised his arm. Gil was scared stiff. He was unable to react. He wanted to draw up his legs or roll out of bed. The lit cigarette dangled from his lips. The charcoal man raised his arm and wagged a long black finger at Gil, waved it back and forth. Small black flecks like soot fell from the man's hand.

Gil finally moved. He jerked the cigarette out of his mouth and flicked it at the man. The cat's eyes blinked, twin yellow lights going out and coming on again. The charcoal man didn't react. But his hat did.

The cat leapt to the bed. It landed in Gil's lap. It felt like fire.

Gil wanted to scream. Instead, he inhaled intense heat when he opened his mouth to take a breath. The air was so hot his tongue sizzled like bacon on a griddle. Gil tried to spit his tongue out of his mouth.

The cat walked up the smoker's chest. Its paws left fiery prints on Gil's bare skin. When the cat reached his face, its whiskers touched his mouth. Gil's lips curled from the heat. He saw the cat briefly. It was black bones and burnt fur. There was no body to it at all. Just eyes, black bones, and burnt fur. Then Gil couldn't see a thing. His eyes fried shut.

His Jerry Lee Lewis hair caught flame. It went up like a great ball of fire.

Gil writhed on the bed. For a few moments, he still had

his legs and feet. They soon burned from the top down, like matchsticks. His toes turned bright red. Like ten glowing cigarette butts, his toes went out, a little puff of smoke lifting from each one. Gil was gone now. He was toast.

Alyssa returned with a glass of water from the bathroom upstairs. If Gil was smoking, she'd throw the water in his face again when he went back to sleep. She turned out the hallway light before pushing the door open. Her bedside lamp lit the room. No one was standing inside.

Gil had a burnt-down cigarette in his mouth. He was dead asleep, his head propped on the pillow. The red glow of the burning cigarette was almost to the filter. Ashes decorated his chin. They looked like black snowflakes.

Alyssa threw the water in his face. Gil didn't wake up.

His not ever waking up again proved a temporary embarrassment for both Alyssa and Gil's wife. The coroner said that he died of smoke inhalation, smoke and heat both. The insides of Gil's mouth were burned.

"He had this trick he did when he got drunk," Alyssa told the police. "He'd flip a burning cigarette inside his mouth and hold it there."

They wanted to know if Gil was a Satan worshiper or if he belonged to a motorcycle gang. Gil, it turned out, had been recently branded from navel to neck with a series of patterns that looked like a cat's paw prints.

Alyssa had never seen the prints before. She told the police she didn't know a thing about them. It was the truth.

"He believed in God," she said. "He never had a motorcycle."

Alyssa took the day off work when Gil was buried. She

didn't go to the funeral. It wouldn't have been right for her to do that, although she wanted to see if they did his hair the way he liked it. She stayed home instead.

Alyssa cried that Gil was gone. She cried herself to sleep. She woke up when the cat ghost kissed her with its whiskers. It felt like a cool mist on her lips.

College Cats

~ ~ ~ ~ ~ ~ ~ ~ ~ ~ ~ ~ ~ ~

Cats can't read your mind, but they can read your body. Cats know before you do when you're almost ready to get something to eat. Cats can see in almost total darkness. They can clearly see you when the lights are out. They know how you behave in your sleep. If you talk in your sleep, your cat is listening to every word, and hearing every breath you take and release. Cats can hear a bat in flight, through a closed window.

Cats know when you are sick and will lie still with you for hours to offer comfort. Some college coeds say a cat can tell when a girl is pregnant by sitting in her lap and listening to the smallest changes inside her body.

Sightings of cat ghosts on college campuses are numerous. In

220　*College Cats*

women's college dorms and sorority houses across the South, for instance, students warn each other of the storied Licks You All Over Cat. Apparently a ghost, or perhaps a demon, the cat shows up when a female college student is asleep. Then it starts licking. The harder you sleep, the harder the ghost cat licks.

Whatever parts of the body it licks will disappear while the coed sleeps.

If the young lady rouses on the first lick or two, she's safe. She can rub the spots, and they come back as good as new. But if she doesn't wake up in time, the student is bound to lose whatever parts of her body have been cat-licked. Because of this, some girls in Southern colleges wear knee socks to bed every night, and long-pants pajamas with pajama tops. Some are said to wear hair caps, sleeping masks, and earmuffs to bed even on the warmest of nights.

The origins of Licks You All Over Cat are impossible to determine. An old campfire tale, perhaps, the story is most often told as a warning to freshmen, away from home for the first time in their lives, not to drink too much. If a girl drinks too much and passes out, she may be entirely gone by morning.

Gentler cats usually teach their humans to recognize the light touch of whisker kisses, given whenever a human has the audacity to oversleep.

Whisker kisses feel like spiders walking on your face.

When cats are happy and content, their whiskers move forward on their faces. When you feel whisker kisses across your cheek or mouth, it's just your cat making sure that you are all right, that you are breathing normally, that the scent of sickness is not upon your breath. A cat needs to know that you are purposely sleeping in, that you are intent on missing out entirely on the utter joy of the first light of dawn sneaking into the house. Of course, an intellectually curious cat will need to know why.

It isn't information, though, that Licks You All Over Cat seeks. It is human flesh.

There is talk of a University of Georgia student named Elaine. She got drunk and fell asleep on her stomach one night. She woke up in the midst of being licked, but not in time. She had to be transported by helicopter in the middle of the night to a hospital for emergency leg transplants. It is told in whispers that the only legs available at the time belonged to an eighty-year-old man who had died in a nursing home.

On another campus, the favorite excuse among members of one sorority when they don't turn in assigned papers on time is to tell the offended professor, "Sorry, cat licked my homework."

While Licks You All Over Cat may be entirely a myth, a ghost cat in one of the women's dorms at the University of South Carolina is not. Coeds who have met the ghost cat often wake up with an "Ouch!" in the middle of its nocturnal visits.

Patterson Hall on the Columbia campus is haunted by the ghost of a kitten that appears from time to time on the ninth floor, but only in December. It is known to crawl into the beds of sleeping students and knead them with its front paws, sometimes biting just a little, other times scratching at the students' shoulders and chests. Though a wee kitten, the ghost animal is strong enough to climb into a bed by snagging sheets or covers that reach over the edge. Once contented with its nibbling, the kitten will purr itself to sleep curled against a sleeper's neck.

The hungry kitten only goes through the motions of finding food. In doing so, it satisfies its hunger. Feeding itself is the only thing the kitten learned to do in its brief life as an earthly being. The kitten is felt, then seen briefly when a student wakes up in the middle of a night's sleep.

"It was on my neck," one Patterson Hall student reported. "When I woke up, it felt like I was wearing a fur."

Fawn Cherie Dwyer, a ninth-floor freshman who woke from the kitten's nocturnal visit, was convinced she had been attacked by a man in her sleep. The signs were obvious to her. Some deviant had broken into her dorm room and taken uncivilized advantage of Fawn Cherie while she slept. She had scratches to prove it. She had her roommate drive her to the hospital emergency room immediately. There, she insisted that the police be called so they could collect DNA to catch the night stalker.

Certain a marauding male was on the prowl in Patterson Hall, Fawn Cherie demanded an investigation be conducted on her behalf. Only God Himself knew what had been done to damage her dignity in the middle of the night. Fawn Cherie was convinced that even in sleep she must have done something to defend herself, whether she remembered it or not. Her fingernails must be checked.

"I was senior drum major in my high school," she said, "and this sort of thing could not happen to me unless I was asleep. I would never allow myself to be scratched like this. I think I may also have been kissed. I must have been given a powerful drug against my knowledge and then slept deeply through the worst of it. If he kissed my ears, you will find DNA there."

The emergency room physician informed her that the shallow bruising on her shoulders was, in fact, the worst of it.

"Spare me no detail," Fawn Cherie demanded. "I want to know everything. Will I be scarred? Will I be capable of bearing children?"

The doctor explained that the bruising was incidental. She had not been physically violated in any other way.

"The bruising is shallow and drawn to the surface, rather than being the deeper bruising caused by blunt force. This injury is more in line with a hickey than an assault."

"I assure you, I do *not* have a hickey on my shoulder!" Fawn Cherie exclaimed. "Or on my neck, for that matter."

"Yes, ma'am," the physician said. He took a deep breath and continued. "Close medical scrutiny reveals tiny scratches to the surface of the skin. The scratches appear to be the imprints of small animal claws."

"Oh, my heavens! Are you saying that I have been kissed by rats?"

"No, I was thinking—"

"I'm going to throw up!"

"Take a deep breath, miss."

He handed her a small, kidney-shaped bedpan, just in case. She set it aside. Fawn Cherie would *not* vomit in front of anyone.

Fawn Cherie's eyes teared. She opened them wide and blinked twice at the emergency room physician. Then she sobbed. The doctor handed her a tissue.

"My entire body must be disinfected. Do you do that

here? My daddy's insurance will cover it." She paused, swallowed hard, tried to stop crying. "Rats are filthy vermin," she said. Fawn Cherie was in college, so she knew these things.

"I was thinking more along the lines of a kitten," the physician said. "And you have not been assaulted by anyone, young lady."

Fawn Cherie Dwyer wanted to be sure.

"Not rats?"

He shook his head.

"No man did this to me?" she asked.

"Not unless he was a leprechaun with a mouth the size of a kitten's. Do you have someone who can take you home?"

"My roommate," she said. "She forgot her shoes and decided to wait in the car."

Fawn Cherie lied about that. Her roommate wore shoes but hadn't had time in the emergency of the moment to fully dress for the drive to the hospital. She was still in her nightgown. No stranger, regardless of his professional accomplishments, needed to be informed of that. Fawn Cherie would see that no possible tint of shame ever tarnished her roommate's sterling reputation through her association with this ugly and repulsive event. Her roommate had been vice president of her high-school student council and was active in debate. The nocturnal indignities had been visited upon Fawn Cherie herself, and she alone would bear their weight.

The Columbia Police Department filed a report of the alleged assault on the ninth floor of Patterson Hall as a false alarm, in agreement with the signed conclusion of the woman reporting the event. Fawn Cherie Dwyer soon after changed dorms. She never owned a cat or dog. Fawn Cherie tried to keep goldfish once but found she could not tolerate the way their mouths moved when they ate.

The history of the Patterson Hall ghost kitten is not a happy one. Linda Mossey, the eldest daughter of a fiery Free Will Baptist minister in a small town near Greenville, was an entering freshman at the University of South Carolina in the late 1960s. She had managed to hide her pregnancy from her conservative parents until college classes. Linda kept almost entirely to herself, spending most of her time in the library stacks, avoiding the normal social life of a college freshman. Her roommate rarely saw her except when Linda was already in bed.

In early December, huddled alone in pain, Linda gave birth in a dorm shower stall. Her baby didn't survive the ordeal. The premature baby was small, and the birth was, though excruciatingly painful for Linda, a relatively simple and direct process. She cut the umbilical cord and managed to heal physically.

Mentally, Linda was a wreck. Heavy with grief for her tiny child, feeling as if she were entirely alone in the world, she quit going to classes. She stopped talking to other students altogether. She hid out behind buildings during class changes, when the campus walkways were crowded with students. Emotionally exhausted and entirely focused on her inner turmoil, Linda was almost run over by a garbage truck one day.

That was the morning a small miracle occurred. Linda found a stray kitten abandoned near the dumpsters behind her residence hall. The little thing was only a week or two old. It had survived its birth, while Linda's own baby hadn't. She hid the kitten in her room and mothered it when no one else was there. Linda hummed lullabies she had learned as a child.

She kept the kitten in a box under her bed when necessary. Other times, she carried it with her, hidden inside her winter coat. Allowing the kitten to cuddle was the only way Linda felt comfort.

Within a week of Christmas break, when she would have to return home for the holidays, Linda could no longer face what she had done. She committed suicide. As an act of devoted companionship, she first strangled her beloved kitten to death.

Linda Mossey is gone now. The details of her suicide are unclear. The kitten, though, cannot rest. It returns to the ninth floor of Patterson Hall every December.

You should never kill a cat, especially a defenseless kitten accustomed to, and deserving of, the milk of human kindness.

JUST WE TWO

Run-Over-Flat Cats

≈ ≈ ≈ ≈ ≈ ≈ ≈ ≈ ≈ ≈ ≈ ≈ ≈ ≈ ≈

Every year at Christmas, Burton Halliday receives one hundred dollars in cash in the mail. There's never a note or a letter. No return address. He thinks he knows who is sending it. And heck, everyone can use a little extra money at Christmas.

Burton piloted an eighteen-wheeler on Highway 78, pulling out of Birmingham, Alabama. His pet cat, Day and Night, snoozed away most of the day in the sleeping loft behind the seats. The growl of the big diesel motor was a giant, comforting purr to Day. The black-and-white cat slept like a tiger when that engine was running. The cat liked sleeping during the day but stayed up with Burton all night, when the truckdriver needed company the most.

One thing truckers see far too much of is road kill. The number of domestic animals dead along American highways is staggering, each one a heartache. A crushed and mangled pet in or at the side of the road sucks the joy right out of a pleasant stretch of gentle downgrade under an otherwise appealing Alabama moon.

Burton found Day and Night as a stray at a rest stop on a divided four-lane. The scraggly creature meowed loudly for food just outside the driver's door of Burton's idling semi. He meowed and meowed until Burton woke up, climbed out of the loft, and opened the driver's door to run the cat off. The cat stayed. The truckdriver didn't mind. He found himself talking to the cat.

"You woke me up from a bad one," he said to the pacing animal.

Burton had been dreaming of his deceased wife. He'd stopped counting the years since she died, but he still dreamed about her almost every night. She was always smiling in his dreams, happy to be with Burton again.

He told the cat all about her. How he had meant to save up money and spend more time with her, spend more time at home. He told the cat how she had always been waiting, day or night, when he came home from the road.

"She'd answer the door with her nightie on," Burton said. "Even if it was noon. She could hear me coming, you see. She could hear that diesel coming up the road before the dog did."

The cat sat still and listened politely. Whenever Burton paused, the stray paced back and forth, meowing to the truckdriver.

"Guess you had family too, at one time," Burton said.

The cat meowed.

"She'd have her nightie on and the bathtub running both.

We had one of those big, deep bathtubs in that old farmhouse. You don't know how badly a trucker wants a long, hot bath after coming off the road. Those truck-stop showers aren't worth a darn when you've gone six days without a bath."

It was an hour or so later when Burton pulled back onto the highway. He brought along the cat. He scooped him up and tossed him into the cab. Burton wasn't through talking.

"We knew each other in high school," the truckdriver said. "But she didn't like me then."

Burton named his cat Day and Night but called him Day for short. At first glance, Day looked like a perfectly black cat that someone had spilt milk on. He was spattered with white everywhere except his tail. The tail was just the reverse. Day's tail was entirely white with a black tip. It looked as if a decent length of daylight had been dipped into a small bottle of night.

Day and night were also the hours they spent together in that truck. Day and night were the hours any long-haul trucker spends on the road, until he stops driving or dies, whichever comes first.

"They say old truckers never die," Burton told the cat. "They just stop talking."

Day was Burton's best friend. The cat would listen to anything.

"I went over to Louisiana and played the horses once," the trucker said. He shook his head in memory of the most expensive three days of his life. "Hey, they say cats can talk to horses. Can you do that?"

Day meowed. Day always talked right back.

"Did I tell you she had a cat? When we first married, she

had this cat. A black cat. I thought it was unlucky. Entirely black, not a speck of color anywhere. Black nose, black whiskers. I never had much to do with that cat."

After a visit to the veterinarian, Day was outfitted with a leash harness. Burton found truck stops that would let the two of them come in and eat. Inside the cab, he strapped a cat kennel to the passenger seat. Small squeaky toys hung from elastic strings over the sleeping loft. Sometimes, Burton would clip a short leash on the harness and let Day ride along sitting atop the kennel. The black cat spattered with white could sit up, stand, stretch, and lie down. Whenever he wanted to, Day could watch the world coming at them through the windshield, or the world going by out the passenger side.

Bugs hitting the windshield always got a loud meow out of Day. The cat chattered like a monkey whenever the windshield wipers came on. At times the truck wasn't rolling, Burton unfastened the short leash and let Day have a romp.

Burton told Day, when they saw run-over animals along the way, not to be sad about it. They'd found a shortcut to heaven, was all. When Burton said that, he was thinking about his wife.

"No, she didn't like me in high school at all. She had a crush on a fellow who already had a girlfriend. She waited till those two got married before she noticed anyone else."

Day licked the back of a paw and waited to hear more. Day was a patient listener. Most cats are.

"She always cried when she saw a dead dog on the highway. She'd just start bawling, then get mad at me because I hadn't told her in time not to look. She'd sit in the car and weep while I walked back and took the poor critter off the road."

He told his cat all the trucker stories about animals that had gotten hit finding ways to get even.

Burton's favorite was the cell phone in the middle of the road.

"Anybody stops to pick up that phone, it starts ringing. Day or night, it's always ringing when you get to it. When a person picks up that phone and answers it, he hears a cat meowing. Then he's hit by a truck he didn't see coming and is dead, just like that."

Burton paused to scratch Day's head a little.

"That's a funny one, Day. I still won't pick up a cell phone in the road if we see one, no matter what you say."

That was just fine by Day.

"Here's another one I can tell you. It's the old lady truck jumper and her cat. Now, that's a scary one."

Day meowed. He liked stories with cats.

"This old lady and her cat are supposed to jump trucks up the highway between Nauvoo and Natural Bridge. Well, the old lady jumps trucks, anyway. The cat does mostly cars. It shows up out of nowhere and plasters itself to the windshield and peers inside with big yellow cat eyes to see who is driving. Then it's gone about as quick as it came."

The poor cat had been killed on the highway by some kids in a car. They kept going after they ran over the cat.

"Didn't stop to see if the cat was dead or anything like that," Burton said.

An old lady in an Oldsmobile behind them saw what happened. She pulled over on the shoulder and got out to see whether the cat was dead or might be helped before it was hit again.

"That cat was dead, all right, and in another ten seconds so was she. Semi got her. It was night, and that driver must have been asleep, to hit an old woman standing in the middle of the road."

Burton shook his head, thinking about it, wondering if it could happen to him.

"Anyway, that big rig slammed right into her at full speed. Knocked her flat and kept going. Driver must have been afraid of the law. Ever since, that same time of night, that lady is supposed to jump right on your truck cab. Would scare you off the road, that would."

Day agreed with a short meow.

"Just like the cat," Burton went on. "She clings to the outside of your cab window to see whether you're the one who ran over her or not. She's all bloody, with broken bones sticking out and everything like that. Her face is smashed, and one of her eyeballs is dangling. She looks right at you with the other one. Then she goes away. Don't know what she'd do if you were the one who killed her. Guess she hasn't found him yet. Maybe he quit driving rigs altogether after that, so she just keeps looking with her one good eye, just at the exact time she was hit on the highway. The bloody old lady keeps looking every night."

Coming out of Birmingham on Highway 78 that night, before the hundred dollars in cash started showing up every Christmas, Burton told Day how his wife liked to drink her tea. He was laughing about it.

"She'd leave her teabag in the cup and just keep drinking her tea. Even if she was dunking a donut into it, she'd leave the teabag in her cup. When the tea was about gone, she'd pour more hot water in and wait a little."

Day started chattering deep in his throat. The cat stood on his kennel with a high, rigid arch to his back. Day yowled, then chattered like a monkey. The cat's whiskers and ears were pinned back.

Burton stopped talking.

The cat stared at the windshield without blinking. He hissed.

It was Day's way of telling Burton that something was about to happen. Day could see farther than most cats. He could see around corners and over hills. Once, they had to come to a screeching stop for traffic just ahead of them waiting out a car wreck. Another time, a dead deer had been in the middle of the road.

This time, this night, the truckdriver knew something was coming up. And coming up fast.

Burton eased off the gas and unhooked Day's leash. The cat disappeared into the loft as soon as he was free. Burton downshifted. The truck lurched into a lower gear. He tapped the top of the kennel three times, and Day came out of the back like a shot and went inside the kennel to wait until it was over.

The truckdriver removed a bit of kibble from his shirt pocket and tossed it inside the kennel before clasping the wire door shut. Day usually meowed a thank-you, but not this time. He curled up in darkness at the back of the kennel and waited.

Burton found yet another gear and had slowed to about thirty-five when he finally saw it. It looked like a wedding cake in the middle of the road. A wedding cake with eyes. Burton hit the airbrakes and went quickly through the final downshifts. The tires barked on the dry pavement.

As the grinding, rapidly decelerating truck jolted forward, Burton saw that what had looked like a wedding cake was actually a white cat. Oddly, the white cat backed up in the road as Burton's truck finally came to a stop. The cat stood on its hind legs, its eyes reflecting in the semi's powerful headlights. Burton had the eighteen-wheeler mostly on the shoulder. He checked the mirrors. Nobody was behind him. The truckdriver tapped on the top of the kennel to let his cat know he would be right back. Day and Night didn't answer.

Burton turned on the flashers, grabbed the flashlight, popped the door, and climbed out. He picked up two flares from the emergency box and ran twenty yards behind the trailer. He ignited the flares in turn, dropping one at his feet and tossing the other as far as he could, farther back along the pavement. Burton returned to the front of the semi as rapidly as he could on two feet.

The white cat was gone.

Burton searched the shoulder and the weeds just beyond with his flashlight. It must have been injured, but not badly enough to be immobilized. He wanted to save that cat. If it dragged itself too far away, where Burton couldn't find it, the cat would lie hidden and might die in the Alabama night.

He ran the wide beam of his flashlight farther into the weeds, finally seeing a pair of eyes. As soon as Burton caught a glimpse of it, the white cat moved in a blur away from the road, up the far side of a shallow roadside ditch. Burton didn't want to cross that ditch but would if he needed to. Checking more deeply into the darkness off the highway, Burton saw something new, a red light near a stand of trees, off to the right a bit. And then another one. It looked like red taillights, but one was on top of the other.

Burton used the flashlight to find a foot route through the ditch. The shoulder was marked with rubber, he saw. And the ditch was shot through with fresh tire cuts. Burton was across the ditch in two jumps, heading with his bouncing light toward the trees, toward the taillights.

Running toward the car in darkness, Burton managed somehow not to fall. There was smoke when he arrived. The air smelled like gasoline.

The car was on its side, two people inside it, a man and a woman. Both were dazed and obviously injured, unable to get the available car door open. Burton clambered up top. It was a difficult maneuver, but Burton was able to open the passenger door. The dome light came on. The man and his wife inside were fairly banged up. The windshield was cracked in three places.

"Let's go," Burton said. "Come on, now!"

The couple stirred.

Burton pushed his full weight against the open door, forcing it back toward the front of the car until the metal bent, locking it in place.

"Take my hand," Burton said to the woman. "Then undo your safety belt."

He got her out and helped her down from the car. He told her to move away. She didn't budge an inch. *She must be in shock*, he thought. The right side of her face was swollen.

The truckdriver climbed back to the open door to pull out the driver. The man was moving around now. Instead of giving Burton his hand, he lifted up a large white cat to the rescuer.

The cat was dead. Burton could tell by looking at it. He knew a dead cat when he saw one. Besides, if the cat were alive, Burton wouldn't have been able to see its ghost in the middle of the road.

If Day and Night hadn't alerted him well in advance, Burton wouldn't have had time to slow down. He wouldn't have been able to stop. He wouldn't have seen the red taillights in the little woods far off the side of the highway.

Burton helped the injured couple move far away from the car. Soon, it burst into flames. The woman could no longer stand. She sat in the wet weeds, watching the car burn. The man's face was covered in blood. Burton found his cell phone and called 911. The state police, the fire department, and two ambulances showed up, filling the darkness with flashing, bright lights.

The woman refused to be put into the ambulance until one of the firemen located and retrieved her cat. She cradled the dead animal to her chest, using her left arm. The other one was broken, as was her collarbone.

It had been the white cat in the road, but Burton told the state trooper that he pulled over because he saw taillights in the woods. Most people didn't understand cats the way Burton did. The truckdriver walked back to his rig with a heavy heart. He pretty much knew what he would find there.

Even though he'd been inside his kennel with the wire door securely latched, Day and Night was gone. Burton's companion wasn't anywhere in the cab.

Day wasn't anywhere on earth.

Day and Night was, and had always been, the combination of two dead cats. The white cat in the wrecked car was one. His wife's long-ago deceased black cat was the other. That night, Burton added one and one together and came up with none.

Burton sat in the driver's seat with the door open. The kennel was empty. The truckdriver poured coffee from his thermos. His hands shook. Burton felt like crying and thought he just might.

He didn't know if cats talked to each other in heaven. There was a good reason, Burton supposed, that his wife's cat had waited to find the right moment to visit him. Maybe dead cats could see the future. *Or maybe*, he thought, *the way we know time on earth isn't the way time works on the other side. Backing up or rolling forward in time, or sitting idle, might all be the same thing, once a body's dead and becomes an angel or a ghost.*

The uniformed trooper in charge of investigating the accident came by to talk to Burton. He stood on the chrome rung below the open driver's door. The trooper had seen much worse along the Alabama highways than what happened that night. But he had rarely seen anything better than what Burton had done.

"Are you all right now?"

"Yes, sir," Burton said. "I believe I am."

"Well, I guess it's time to move along. We have your name and address if we need to get in touch. I'll take care of the flares for you."

Burton nodded.

"Oh," the trooper added, "one more thing. The man in the car wanted you to have this. He said he wished it was more."

The trooper handed Burton five crumpled twenty-dollar bills.

Burton drove away that night as lonely as the first Christmas without his wife. He could smell the burnt car inside his nose. He could taste it. He drove toward Nauvoo, working it out in his head the way things had happened. He was sure now that cat ghosts talked to one another on the other side. And Burton was certain beyond doubt that Day and Night was gone the moment the white cat appeared in the road.

The trucker bought dual chrome outlines of cats for his mud flaps.

His first day off at home, Burton Halliday visited the local animal shelter.

"A cat then, is it?" the attendant asked him.

"Yes, ma'am. I'm looking for a stray that talks, if you happen to have one that needs a home."

The lady laughed. It was an awfully nice sound to Burton.

"Got one that's been waiting just for you," she said. "When it comes to talking, this one is a harp on roller skates, like to drive us all insane. It squawks, chatters, yodels, and plays the drums."

"That one, please," Burton said.

He smiled at the lady. She had nice eyes and was about his age. He wished he knew more women like this one. Women who laughed. When Burton was younger, he liked to dance. He'd dance around the living room to songs on the radio. His legs were older now, cramped up from sitting in the cab of that truck all day and all night. Perhaps it was about time he got around to dancing again.

"If you want a noisy cat, you two are going to have a real fine time."

"If you wouldn't be doing anything for dinner tonight, I

could fix that for you," Burton said.

The woman blushed.

"Well, sir," she finally said, "my name is Carole Jean Anderson." She held out her hand. "And I already know yours, Burton Halliday."

"Yes, ma'am. It's a pleasure."

The woman looked warm and soft. Her hair was blond and her eyes crystal blue. She knew his name, so she must have been someone he'd met before. He didn't remember it.

"You know, Burton, I was friends with your wife before she died. I talked to you at the funeral and told you to call me anytime you didn't feel like being alone."

"Sorry to say, I don't remember," Burton confessed. "I wasn't paying attention then. Most of me died when she did, and it's taken a long time for me to—"

"Hush, now," she told him. Carole Jean held up a finger to his lips. "Don't apologize. I understand."

He asked Carole Jean if she liked to dance. She said she surely did.

Burton paid the adoption fees and named his new cat C. B.

"Have I got a story to tell you about cats," he told his new pet. "I don't really know where it begins, C. B. Did you know my wife had a cat when I first married her? Now, it was black. I'd be ashamed to say the name Jesus if that cat wasn't black all over. The blackest cat you ever saw."

C. B. meowed and waited to hear the end of this one.

A Patch of Fog

~ ~ ~ ~ ~ ~ ~ ~ ~ ~ ~ ~ ~ ~

People say there are witches on Mount Rogers. Others say they are just old ladies with cats. All agree, though, that wild horses are up there. And fog.

This time of year, the fog rolls down from Mount Rogers at night, fills the mountain hollows, and spills across Interstate 81 into the edges of Marion, Virginia. The fog from Mount Rogers carries a strong spruce scent. By morning, most of it has lifted, pulled back to the mountain like misty outstretched fingers being drawn into a fist. Those who rise early enough in Marion and step outdoors to start their day are apt to say they are smelling the mountain as the last scented wisps of fog quickly disappear.

Cindy Evans smelled the mountain. The twenty-seven-year-old was late for work. What she wanted to smell were coffee and a cigarette.

She'd slept right through the sound of her alarm. Cindy didn't have time to make coffee that morning, and she'd run out of cigarettes the night before. She tied her hair into a ponytail and quickly jabbed her legs inside the same pair of permanently creased black slacks she'd worn to work two days earlier. She pulled a blouse off a hanger in the closet and slipped it on. She found her shoes, grabbed a toothbrush and her purse, and was out the door.

Cindy would have to stop at the little store in Sugar Grove, even though she didn't have time for it. She needed coffee and cigarettes. And she needed to visit the ladies' room. She'd forgotten to do that before leaving the house.

She heard the wild ponies holler from a meadow where they roamed a little higher up the mountain. Someone camping on the Appalachian Trail must have startled them. Hikers always approached the wild horses until they got close enough to make them holler. Cindy's grandfather had told her that the ponies hollered when a panther was near. She didn't believe any of that. Mountain panthers were extinct in Virginia, and had been for generations.

Cindy hated her job. She hated even more being late to a job she hated. This morning, she hated the mountain, and she hated the wild horses, too. They could just go live somewhere else, for all she cared.

She stuck her toothbrush in her mouth and tried to button her blouse with one hand as she drove her Ford Mustang through the S-curves in the road. She came to a complete stop at the intersection with Flat Ridge Road and managed to get two buttons closed. It was a steep uphill turn onto Flat Ridge, and a blind one. Cindy rolled the driver's window down to get a clear view of the sharp turn in the road to her left. You could never really tell if a car was coming. She usually counted to three, then drove onto Flat Ridge anyway.

At the count of one, an emerald hummingbird showed up at the tip of her nose. It flew in through the window, looked at Cindy, hovered just over the red handle of the toothbrush sticking out of her mouth, and buzzed out again, like a bee. By the time she said "Two," the wing-whir of iridescent hummingbird was gone. Hummingbirds were messengers, her grandmother said. They brought good news.

Cindy wished they brought coffee and cigarettes.

"Three!" She pulled quickly onto Flat Ridge Road.

As soon as she did, she saw it. A patch of fog stood in the road. A patch of fog the size of a person. Cindy blinked twice. It looked like an old woman, and then it looked like fog again. She bit down on her toothbrush's bristles and drove right through the fog. She had no choice. She didn't have time to stop for fog, no matter whose shape it was in.

She felt cool mist brush across her face. Cindy didn't realize what she'd done. A ghost lived inside that standing figure of fog. The ghost was an old lady with an important errand to run.

On the other side of the patch of fog, Cindy felt odd all over. She felt strangely different from head to toe. She felt old. She couldn't see as well. Her peripheral vision was gone. Either that or fog had moved in all around her. She slowed down. Her foot barely reached the pedal. She pushed her face closer to the steering wheel. Her hands ached.

Cindy took the toothbrush out of her mouth. It hurt her gums to have it there. She meant to drop it in the passenger seat next to her purse, but her fingers didn't cooperate with the plan. The toothbrush fell from her hand and clattered on the floorboard.

Driving slowly to the little store in Sugar Grove, she could barely see over the steering wheel and had to use both hands to turn the wheel in order to pull into the parking lot. Cindy was a little late in pushing her foot on the brake pedal, and the Mustang eased into the yellow-painted concrete post in front of the store. The front of the car crunched, but just a little. No real harm. And frankly, Cindy didn't notice what she had done.

She slipped her arm through the strap of her purse and gingerly climbed out of the car. Cindy walked across the small portion of parking lot between her and the door into the little store. The purse was heavy on her arm. Her shoes were too small. Her feet and ankles hurt. A stabbing pain shot through her left hip with every step. She left the car door open.

A dull pain was in her neck, and she couldn't raise her head all the way. She looked at her shoes and wondered why they were so small. Cindy couldn't imagine how she'd ever gotten them on. Maybe she had slept in them and never taken them off.

She managed somehow to get inside the store. A blurry fat man stood behind the counter just inside the door. Cindy had to cock her head sideways to look at him.

My, oh, my! He was fat, all right, the fattest man she'd ever seen. She remembered his name was Mike Wilson. They'd gone to high school together. Cindy liked him well enough. Mike was the only person in her graduating class who had a worse job than she did. But he was fat and dumb. What was her excuse?

Cindy started to say good morning but forgot his name. Was it Mike?

"You left your lights on," the fat man said.

I'm wearing my tights wrong? Cindy thought. Whatever was this fat man talking about? She wasn't wearing tights. She hadn't worn tights since taking ballet lessons in the fourth grade.

Cindy knew what she'd come for but didn't know where in the store to find it.

"Cath foof!" she shouted at the fat man.

"Next to the dog food. Right there at the end of the aisle you're on."

White bear's in the bend of Lake Huron? Cindy didn't care where bears lived in Lake Huron. And she sure didn't give a twit what color they were. Had that fat man called her dog poop? She'd have one of the men in her family cane him but good if he did it again.

"I goth no teef!" Cindy said to herself, shouting it. She brought her hand to cover her mouth.

"I neef cath foof!" Cindy tried again, louder this time. The top of her thighs turned warm. Cindy had wet her pants a little. She was glad she was wearing the black ones. "Half-en-half!" she added.

The fat man carried dry and canned cat food to her car. And a small carton of half-and-half. Cindy managed to set her purse on the counter. She reached inside for her debit card and brought out a fat bundle of dollar bills she'd never seen before. She held the loose money with her thumb crossed over her palm. Her hand shook. Her fingers wouldn't work right. When Cindy lifted her thumb, the bills fluttered onto the counter like a deck of spilled cards.

Mike Wilson shuffled the silver certificates and set them aside. He'd seen old folks come into the store with antique money lots of times, maybe twice a week or more. They must have cans of old money hidden everywhere up in those little houses on Mount Rogers. He handed Cindy back a few bills, using regular ones. He rounded off the pennies to her benefit and set fifty-five cents in change on the counter. She left it there.

The fat man helped Cindy to her car, holding her left arm as if it were broken. Her knees barely worked at all.

The engine was still running. Cindy got her purse into the passenger seat and herself behind the wheel. The fat man closed the car door for her.

"Thore smelf life pee!" she told him through the rolled-down window. The fat man should do something about that if he expected repeat customers. Cindy would drive to Marion the next time she needed things. She had a friend from high school who clerked in the grocery store there. Or maybe that was Sugar Grove. She couldn't remember which right now. It didn't matter anyway. The boy was fat and dumb and of no account to her one way or the other.

The car seemed to drive itself once she got the gearshift out of Park, the way it does when you're daydreaming and it takes you exactly where you're going without your having to think about it at all. The Mustang didn't take Cindy to work that morning. Instead, she rode slowly back up the mountain, turning here or there with her hands on the wheel. Her vision was fogged. She ended up on a gravel road high on the mountain. The gravel road changed into a grassy lane.

She parked in front of a small house. A hummingbird was in the yard. Cindy felt a little younger here, younger than when she'd been in the store. She remembered she was late for work. She dumped her purse out on the passenger seat to find her cell phone. She'd call to let them know she was running behind.

Her cell phone wasn't there. She must have left it at home. Then she looked at the little house with the sagging porch roof in front and thought this might be home instead. The key to the front door was on the seat with the other items spilled from her purse. Cindy wasn't sure how she knew that, but she did. She picked up the key and carefully made three trips from the car, each time setting a different bag from the store on the porch.

Inside, she found the house completely furnished. It was clean as a pin. A pair of prescription eyeglasses was on the dining-room table. Cindy picked the glasses up and put them on. She could see a little better then.

The cat in the kitchen was a handsome young thing. It paced the floor, waiting to be fed.

It moved its mouth as if it were speaking, but Cindy couldn't hear a thing.

"Your name is Biscuits," she said to the cat. When it wasn't a person who was listening, Cindy's words sounded as normal as when she had all her teeth.

A second cat came into the kitchen. Cindy had expected it, too.

"Good morning, Gravy," she said to the cat.

Biscuits and Gravy, the two house cats, took turns walking between Cindy's legs, rubbing the lengths of their bodies against her. Cindy's legs felt better. Her feet seemed a little less swollen.

Cindy turned on the coffee maker. It had been readied the night before. A half-full bottle of red food coloring was on the counter. She set it aside and used the electric opener to pretend to open a can of cat food. Biscuits and Gravy meowed like crazy when she used the can opener. Cindy smiled, listening to the cats compete for loudest breakfast yowl. She could hear them now. Being with the cats made her feel more comfortable in her body.

She pulled open the tab-top cans and fed the cats. Her fingers worked fine now.

Cindy filled a five-gallon dispenser with fresh water. The dispenser was propped up on the floor over an orange plastic bowl. Cindy knew exactly what it was for. She filled the perpetual cat feeder with dry kibble and added two drops of red food coloring to a pan of sugar water sitting cold on the stove. She brought the twin hummingbird feeders in from the front porch and poured red sugar water inside each one. Enough remained in the pan for another day.

Through the kitchen window, she watched a pair of wild horses in the grassy field behind the house. They looked just right to her, even after she took off her glasses. The horses looked perfect. They looked at peace. Cindy poured half-and-half into a mug of fresh, hot coffee.

Biscuits and Gravy walked out onto the sloping porch with Cindy. The cats stretched, then lazily strolled off into the yard.

They'd return soon, she knew. The mountain morning would be officially through when they did. Likely as not, Gravy would bring back a mole or a mouse and drop it at Cindy's feet.

Setting down the mug of steaming coffee, Cindy went back into the house and retrieved a hairbrush from the bedside stand. On her way back out, she picked up the crocheted lap blanket from the couch. Sitting in one of the two slat-seat rockers on the porch, Cindy removed the band from her ponytail. She brushed her hair with one hand while sipping the best cup of coffee she'd ever had in her life. She didn't think once about wanting a cigarette.

Mist lifted from the yard, disappearing as the sun warmed the mountain air. Cindy heard a whirring sound by her left ear. Suddenly, the hummingbird hovered in front of her face. Her grandmother said hummingbirds were messengers, but this one didn't have a thing to say. It darted to first one feeder, then the other. Soon, a second hummingbird joined it.

The twin buccaneers of buzz battled each other for access to both of the feeders. *Just like people*, Cindy thought. She laughed. She had a feeder for each of them, but that wasn't enough. The water was always sweeter in the other bird feeder.

Cindy was listening to the sound of water rushing around rocks in a nearby mountain branch when she heard a short whinny to the side of the porch. One of the wild horses was coming into the yard. It shook its thick mane once, as if to ask permission. Then, ignoring Cindy, the horse walked slowly forward, munching tufts of grass. Cindy wished she had eyes as pretty as those of the horse. She could count its eyelashes from where she sat.

The hummingbirds left and came back, each repeatedly trying to trick the other into finding another place in the woods to feed.

While Cindy was finishing her second mug of coffee, the cats returned. Cindy went inside to dispose of the mouse. Biscuits and Gravy came with her. Cindy moved the glasses from the kitchen counter to the dining-room table, where she had found them. She tidied up the house a bit and prepared the coffee maker for its next use.

Cindy sat on the couch and played with the cats. Her time here was over. The last wisp of fog had lifted from the mountain. She sighed. She smiled. She didn't have a single ache or complaint. She closed the door behind her and breathed in deeply. She smelled the mountain. It smelled of spruce trees and jasmine grass. It smelled of running water and tangled vines. It smelled wild, and it smelled sweet.

≈ ≈ ≈ ≈

At the store in Sugar Grove, the fat man pushed a package of cigarettes across the counter.

Cindy Evans snatched it up. She was running late.

"Your hair looks nice today," Mike Wilson said. He stared at her chest, as usual.

"Yours would, too," she told him, "if you had any left on top."

Cindy raced into Marion. In minutes, she backed her Mustang into one of the parking slots at work. Hurrying around the front of the car, ready to break into a trot, she stopped dead in her tracks. The front bumper was crunched. She frowned and pulled the cell phone from her purse. She called her house.

"Steve, if you ever drive my car again without asking, and it isn't an honest-to-God emergency, you can pile up your clothes and leave right then," she said. "Because I'm kicking you out."

She hurried inside, ready to apologize for being late. Mrs. Wilson sat at the front desk under a stack of gray curls that looked as if they were painted in place. She stared at Cindy with her mouth open. Cindy looked up at the clock.

"What?" the twenty-seven-year-old asked. "I still have two minutes before I'm late for work."

"Your blouse is unbuttoned, dear," the older lady said with a sniff.

"Oh, that," Cindy said. She tried not to blush. "I stopped at the store in Sugar Grove. Your son must have stared it open."

The Cat
in the Well

≈ ≈ ≈ ≈ ≈ ≈ ≈ ≈ ≈ ≈ ≈ ≈ ≈

Bruce Bagzis couldn't sleep and didn't want to travel. It was silly to be this worried about a cat. He'd been phoning his wife every few hours. Normally, Charleston was his favorite city to visit on business. This morning, he didn't want to be there. He didn't want to be anywhere.

He'd driven the rental car from the airport down Interstate 26. Somehow, he had drifted onto the Mark Clark Expressway and circled half the city, coming into town across the Cooper River Bridge, all 13,000 feet of it suspended under two diamond-shaped cable towers. The towers reach 575 feet in height. He drove under both of them and barely noticed.

Sugar was depressed, the veterinarian said. And she was about to die because of it. Bruce didn't know how a cat could sit there day after day and then die. But that's exactly what appeared to be happening. Sugar had been his daughter's cat. Hannah named her. Sugar stayed with Hannah in the hospital, kept the young girl company through chemotherapy and worse. It was two months since Hannah passed, and now the cat had decided she would die, too. Just like that.

"Cats hold out hope when someone is gone," the vet had told Bruce and his wife. "She's convinced now that your daughter is not coming back."

After their daughter died, Sugar sat in Hannah's chair and meowed. The white cat slept in Hannah's bed and meowed every ten minutes through the night. Sugar roamed the house looking for Hannah. She tried to coax Bruce and his wife, Cheryl, into looking for their daughter. They had nowhere to look but the graveyard.

Bruce cried about it. Cheryl cried, too. They cried about Hannah, but they had been doing that all along. Sugar's depression was something new. She quit eating. She quit grooming, and her coat went dull. Her eyes seemed to see nothing. Sugar lost interest in everything. She just sat there and waited to die. The vet gave them pills to stimulate her appetite. That approach didn't work.

Bruce cried because Sugar was the last living thing they had of Hannah's. Sugar held the family together through it all. When Hannah died, Sugar stayed with them through the night while Bruce and Cheryl wept for the loss of their child. Cancer takes its toll. In the end, the young girl was tired of it, exhausted beyond what a child should ever know, really. In the end, they were prepared to lose Hannah, to let her go.

Sugar, Bruce feared, was all that held him and Cheryl together now. Sugar was the remaining bit of life that made the house bearable. If Sugar died, Bruce would have to move out of that house. He'd have to leave Hannah's house. He wondered if Cheryl would come with him. Bruce Bagzis couldn't sleep.

The sky in Charleston looked the same as the ocean to Bruce.

After Hannah died, he went back to work. This was his first trip for the company. He thought Charleston would be perfect. He thought he would walk the streets of the old city and remember Hannah in a fond way, think of her as being somehow well now, though gone, think of her being alive and happy again, in his heart.

Charleston was supposed to be his time alone with his deceased daughter.

Now, all he could think about was that cat. If Sugar died, it would be the cat telling Bruce and Cheryl that they should, too. Maybe that's what parents were supposed to do.

His meeting was later that day at the Maison Du Pré. Simple stuff, really. Just signing contracts in person, instead of through the mail. Might be a pencil change or two in the margin, then a handshake, a few friendly words. It was the way things worked in the South. Might as well do your contracts with firms in New York City, if you wanted to put everything into Fed Ex packets and never meet the people with whom you conducted your business affairs.

Bruce left his room at the Du Pré. He couldn't just sit there like Sugar and stare at the wall. It wasn't quite daylight yet when he found the coffee shop on East Bay Street. He got the largest they had, added sugar, and put three creams in the pocket of his sports coat. He bought a muffin but ended up cramming that in his pocket as well. He thought he would walk down Washington and Concord streets to Waterfront Park but ended up on Anson Street instead. Walking against the one-way traffic made him somehow feel more comfortably alone.

"You-all can go where you want to," Bruce said to no one at all. "I'm going this way."

Soon, he was meandering on one-way cross streets for a couple of blocks, then wandering back south another block or two, turning when he felt like it. He barely touched his coffee. Bruce liked Charleston, its buildings much lower than most cities. You could see church spires everywhere. They were the tallest things around.

It felt like it was going to rain, but then Charleston always felt that way.

Palmetto palms were everywhere. They were cute trees, but this morning they seemed uninviting. You couldn't stand under one for shade, after all. And you didn't want to lean against one either. Their trunks looked scaly to Bruce. You wouldn't want to put your shoulder or your hand there.

He found a block with massive old oaks. The airy Spanish moss hanging from the tree branches looked like ruined lace in the first light of dawn, looked like shrouds just the right size for Hannah's dolls. Charleston had been so inviting and so charming the other times Bruce visited. On his honeymoon, for starters. It was supposed to be just the place for his first trip away from home since Hannah died.

That morning, though, the little city streets with their columned houses and window-shuttered businesses weren't inviting at all. Cobblestone streets and paths lay here and there, and fountains and gardens, but the whole of Charleston seemed to be shut away from the streets by tall hedges, iron fences and gates, and pastel-painted or gray stucco block walls. You had to have a permit or a key to sit down anywhere at all. Being in Charleston felt wrong.

Bruce decided to head on back toward the grass at Waterfront Park. If he sat there, maybe the ocean would have something to say to him of an early morning in Charleston. He found a shortcut through a narrow paved alley, then realized too late it turned sharply to the right. Before he knew it, the little alleyway dead-ended. The wrought-iron gate hanging at the end of the alley was open.

He supposed he could be arrested if anybody minded his being there. That was okay, since the police were polite in Charleston. He would move on if someone asked him to. Inside the gate was a courtyard. A low brick wall ran across the back. Pieces of slate covered the ground. A small stone fountain stood in the middle. It wasn't turned on. Coins were in the bottom of it, where children had made wishes.

Bruce wondered what he would wish for, if he could wish for anything other than Hannah's not having died so sick and so young. What was it people wished for? Wealth, fame, happiness, love.

He sat on the brick wall and felt like crying. That was nothing new. Bruce set his coffee down next to him, pulled off the sip-through cap, and poured in a cream. The coffee had turned cold. He probably wouldn't drink it. The sun was fully awake now. It shone in separate beams of light among the trees. Birds, already finished with most of their morning singing, moved in the branches.

He heard water. It sounded to Bruce as if something splashed behind him.

Leaning backwards over the brick wall, he found himself staring at a crescent-shaped hole in the ground. The hole was mostly covered by a round lid made from pieces of thick boards. Bruce turned around and leaned over the wall on both hands to get a better view. The wooden cover had partially slipped aside atop a circle of bricks. The bricks were much older than those used to build the garden wall.

He heard something splash again.

It was a well, Bruce realized. He had been taught as a child to stand back from wells. His grandmother told him that a cannibal witch named Annie Greenteeth lived at the bottom of wells. She had long, sharp teeth and ate children who leaned their faces over wells. Her bony arms were long enough to reach to the top, no matter how deep the well might be. She hooked her long, crooked fingers into peering faces and pulled them in. If that wasn't scary enough, Annie Greenteeth had bad breath, his grandmother said. Like cooked cabbage and onions.

It was a well, and something moved inside it. Something splashed.

Bruce was over the wall in a flash. Bending over the well, he used both hands to pull the cover back. Two copper-colored eyes looked up at him. A tiny wet head cocked from side to side. The eyes didn't plead for rescue. They were curious over who Bruce might be. He reached for the animal, which was treading water.

The soaked cat leapt up the side of the well on its own and was out quickly. It looked like a tan otter. It bounded to the top of the brick wall and stood on all fours, shaking water from its fur in a series of head-to-tail shudders. Then it stretched. The cat was still thoroughly wet and looked distressed to Bruce. It was skinny, starved. The cat looked miserable wet.

Bruce took off his sports jacket and laid it across the wall. He returned to where he'd been sitting before. He took off his tie and unbuttoned his shirt. In want of company, the wet cat walked the wall. Bruce called to it. It knocked over his coffee. Bruce pulled off his shirt and wrapped the cat in it. He rubbed the shirt gently over the animal, its head sticking out. As he toweled off the cat, she purred.

Then she walked away from him. Both left feet forward, then both right. She stopped to smell the spilt coffee. The cat chose a spot on the wall in sunlight. She lay out to her full length and stared at Bruce.

"You could say thank you," Bruce said.

He flapped his shirt in the air, hoping to dry it. Then he spread it out on his half of the brick wall. Shirtless, he slipped his jacket on and draped his tie loosely around his neck.

"We both look like idiots," he said.

The cat agreed and immediately began to groom her face with her paws. She was the color of sand, he noticed. Two colors of sand, actually, in a faint pattern of tabby stripes. Bruce remembered the muffin in his pocket. He peeled the top off it and brought it to the cat. He set it in front of her. She stretched her head forward for a quick smell, then drew back and continued combing her fur into place.

She stopped once to stare at Bruce, blinking. He stood in front of her. One color was sand, he decided, and the other was cream.

He remembered the two creams in his jacket pocket. He got one out, fumbled the top off, and held the cream in front of the cat. He held it in his fingers so she could lap up the sweet milk without knocking the container over with her tongue. It wasn't good for cats to have much cream, he knew. But she wanted it.

As soon as she was through, she groomed her face again, cleaning her whiskers. Bruce leaned against the wall and watched. He had nowhere to go. He thought they should be friends, his having saved her life and all.

"What are you going to eat today?" he asked.

The cat rolled onto her back in the morning sun. She was confident, afraid of nothing, he realized.

"A mouse, maybe? Grasshoppers?"

The cat meowed. She seemed to want her belly rubbed. Bruce was hesitant. Cats won't often let people touch their bellies. Sugar sure wouldn't. He tickled the cat's soft belly fur with two fingers, then petted her gently. She purred. The cat had what she wanted.

In a moment, she slipped from under his hand and sat upright on the wall. The cream tabby cat sat beside Bruce and stared at the fountain in the middle of the courtyard. She meowed loudly, waited, then meowed again. Bruce stared at the fountain, remembering the coins he'd seen there when he first walked by. He crossed his arms. The cat meowed a third time.

"What would I wish for?" Bruce said out loud. "I guess I'd wish for more sleep."

The cat waited.

"Oh, I know. I wish that Sugar wouldn't die." It was killing Bruce to watch Hannah's cat go through that. It was killing him to watch Cheryl watch the cat slowly die. "You wouldn't do that," Bruce said to the cat sitting next to him. "You were in a well paddling around like a drowning rat, and you're not depressed."

The well cat didn't say anything.

Bruce's cell phone sounded. He flipped it open. It was Cheryl. He pushed the button.

"You're not going to believe this, Bruce. Sugar is eating. Right now. She got me out of bed, pawing my face like she used to, ran straight to the kitchen, and begged for breakfast! She begged, Bruce. She begged."

"You're kidding me!"

She wasn't kidding. Sugar ate and was marching around the kitchen, waiting for Cheryl to settle down with a cup of coffee and pay some attention to her.

Bruce beamed inside. He told Cheryl everything was okay on his end. He yawned. He told his wife he couldn't wait to be home. He'd leave as soon as the contracts were signed. He would tell her about the cat in the well later. Sugar was the news of the morning.

Bruce closed and pocketed his phone. The sun was burning now. It was hot. Bruce felt himself begin to sweat. *Welcome to Charleston*, he thought.

The sand-and-cream tabby from the well stretched out in the sun, then curled on her side, feet over the edge of the brick wall. She closed her eyes. Bruce walked over to retrieve his shirt. His sports jacket was heavy and hot. He folded his shirt over his arm. He picked up the coffee cup and put its lid back on. He'd find a proper place to dispose of it. The cat opened her copper eyes and meowed again.

"I wish I were in Bermuda shorts and a tank top," Bruce said.

It was his third wish, and with that the cat from the well was gone.

Bruce walked to the Maison Du Pré wearing a bright yellow sleeveless T-shirt over a pair of green-and-maroon Bermuda shorts. He still had his shoes and socks, but his dress shirt, his tie, his slacks, and his sports jacket were gone.

Charleston looked prettier this time around. He strolled under the welcoming shade of the grand old oaks. The palmetto palms leaned this way and that, as if to wave hello. The houses seemed to nod in agreement with the weather. Cars moved by at reasonable speeds, demonstrating perfect Southern etiquette. The ocean rested in the comfort of a brand-new day. A church bell rang.

He emptied his pockets in his room at the Du Pré. Everything was there. Wallet, checkbook, cell phone, car keys. He meant to call Cheryl, but he fell asleep instead. He slept through the meeting. He slept through the phone's ringing. He slept through the polite knocks on his door. It was the first time he'd slept for more than an hour or two since Hannah's death.

Bruce Bagzis dreamed he'd found Aladdin's lamp, and was awake in time for supper.

Author's Afterword

If you would like to share your ghost experiences, I may be reached by email at randyrussell@aol.com. You are also invited to visit my website at GhostFolk.com.

I regularly present ghost-lore programs for groups both large and small across the South. These presentations often include hours of first-person ghost encounters from my oral library of never-to-be-published true ghost stories. I am an annual presenter of the week-long Ghost Seminar at the North Carolina Center for the Advancement of Teaching.